THE ROBINSON WAY

A Guide for Raising Responsible Kids

DR. JAMES J. CUNNINGHAM

Copyright © 2021 Dr. James J. Cunningham.

All rights reserved. No part of this book may be used or reproduced by any means, graphic, electronic, or mechanical, including photocopying, recording, taping or by any information storage retrieval system without the written permission of the author except in the case of brief quotations embodied in critical articles and reviews.

This book is a work of non-fiction. Unless otherwise noted, the author and the publisher make no explicit guarantees as to the accuracy of the information contained in this book and in some cases, names of people and places have been altered to protect their privacy.

Archway Publishing books may be ordered through booksellers or by contacting:

Archway Publishing
1663 Liberty Drive
Bloomington, IN 47403
www.archwaypublishing.com
844-669-3957

Because of the dynamic nature of the Internet, any web addresses or links contained in this book may have changed since publication and may no longer be valid. The views expressed in this work are solely those of the author and do not necessarily reflect the views of the publisher, and the publisher hereby disclaims any responsibility for them.

Any people depicted in stock imagery provided by Getty Images are models, and such images are being used for illustrative purposes only. Certain stock imagery © Getty Images.

ISBN: 978-1-4808-9791-5 (sc)
ISBN: 978-1-4808-9792-2 (e)

Library of Congress Control Number: 2020920474

Print information available on the last page.

Archway Publishing rev. date: 1/4/2021

To: Phyllis, Mary Beth, Kathy, and Jim
and with great gratitude to Dr. Joseph Robinson

Thanks also to Mary Ellen Pichiarello for her invaluable assistance and loyal support and to Auraleah Grega for her skillful editing.

CONTENTS

Introduction ix

Chapter 1   Responsibility, Discipline, Honesty, and Love 1
Chapter 2   Intelligent Parenting 15
Chapter 3   It's (Almost) All in the Family 30
Chapter 4   Family of Origin Survey 60
Chapter 5   Psychosocial Development 74
Chapter 6   The Robinson Way 90
Chapter 7   Choices and Habits 111
Chapter 8   Overparenting and How To Avoid It 124
Chapter 9   Additional Considerations and Observations 140
Chapter 10   Summary and Final Thoughts 160

Appendix 171
References 175

INTRODUCTION

The idea of writing a book about parenting has been alternately in the foreground or background of my mind for some time. I have been working with children, adolescents, and families for several decades. I had offered my share of advice and recommendations to parents, groups, and other professionals, but I had never attempted to present my ideas to a broader audience.

It was while I was conducting workshops for teachers and counselors at a regional conference in Northeastern Pennsylvania a number of years ago that the idea of writing a book began to germinate. The keynote speaker for the conference was Dr. William Glasser. He is the founder of an approach to treatment known as Reality Therapy. I was well aware of his work and I agree with many of his concepts. Briefly, Glasser's approach stresses the need for individuals to accept full responsibility for their behavior and to act accordingly. When first introduced, his beliefs were quite different than the more widely accepted Freudian concepts. In the Freudian view, neurosis resulted primarily from being overly inhibited and repressed emotionally and behaviorally. Individuals needed to learn to be free from these inhibitions in order to gratify their instinctual needs. Glasser disagreed. He felt that true need fulfillment came from doing what is realistic and responsible. His theories will be further discussed in subsequent chapters.

Consistent with the theme of the workshop, I was outlining some strategies which teachers and counselors could employ in the classroom and in their work with parents. The primary objective was to help children achieve a higher level of self-discipline and self-control. Attendees at the conference were from several school districts which were relatively close to each other geographically. I had cited several examples of what I considered to be self-disciplined "responsible" students. In comments at breaks and after my presentation, teachers from more than one district told me these responsible children sounded like "Robinson kids." I inquired about this and found that these children were not part of a very large family but rather all patients of the same pediatrician, Dr. Joseph Robinson. Remarkably, teachers told me they could easily pick out the "Robinson kids" from their peers. Not only was their behavior excellent, they were also happy and high achieving. I resolved at that moment to learn more about this man and his work.

When I contacted Dr. Robinson, I was impressed by his self-effacing and "down to earth" manner. He was reluctant to accept a great deal of credit for helping children and parents. He saw this as his responsibility. He told me that when he finished his pediatric residence, he felt comfortable in dealing with children's health problems, but he had no idea of how to work with parents in terms of guiding them toward good child rearing practices. He decided that a significant part of his role of pediatrician was to provide parent education. He kept his practice rather small and required a commitment from parents to accept his recommendations. There is a good deal of evidence that parents who made this commitment were quite pleased with the results.

Not long after meeting Dr. Robinson, I was asked to conduct a series of workshops for public health nurses. These nurses were assigned to working with parents of infants and children from lower socioeconomic level families. I was able to talk Dr. Robinson into being a co-presenter at these workshops. It was a wonderful learning experience for both the nurses and myself. I later had him as a guest lecturer in my classes at the University of Scranton where he was very well received. We collaborated on other projects as well and became good friends. He frequently said that we should write a book about parenting. We made a couple of feeble attempts, but our schedules and my lack of self-discipline stymied our plan. Unfortunately, he passed away several years ago. I believe that Dr. Robinson's knowledge and experience can be very helpful to parents and needs to be available to them. I will present his ideas in detail in a later chapter of this book.

As noted above, I accept the primary responsibility for not having written this book sooner. However, I believe I was also hesitant to begin for other reasons as well.

Even a cursory review of the literature reveals a very large number of books on parenting. Do we really need one more? The quality of the advice and ideas for parents varies greatly. Some offer quick, easy solutions and characterize parenting as a very straightforward and easy process. Others do offer psychologically sound advice and helpful strategies for problem solving. However, there are a great deal of conflicting opinions as to how best to parent along with what I consider to be some very bad advice. Telling parents how to raise their kids has long been one of the favorite activities of many "helping" professionals. Often this is done in a somewhat self-righteous, judgmental manner. While this may make the professionals feel good, those feelings may not be shared by the recipients of this advice. Blaming and criticizing parents can, and often does, lead to increased feelings of guilt, anxiety, and inadequacy. I learned long ago that telling people to do what they are unable to do is not very "helpful."

After reviewing several of the more widely accepted parenting books, I concluded that none offered a truly comprehensive presentation of all aspects of the parenting process. The goal of this book is to present a more comprehensive overview of parenting in a way that could help parents become more competent and confident in their actions. As a parent and grandparent, I realize the importance of effective parenting and the rich intrinsic gratification it can bring. As a psychologist I am also well aware of the pain, suffering, and multiple costs associated with irresponsible behavior.

It is my sincere hope that after reading this book parents will have a greater understanding of how to promote responsible behavior in their children. However, just knowing what to do is not enough. This is where I feel the currently available information falls short. I believe parents need to be fully aware of the larger context in which parenting occurs and the various barriers and hazards which can prevent them from acting in a way that promotes responsible behavior. It is only when these issues are understood and resolved that we can become truly responsible parents.

I was also hesitant to begin writing this book because my formal experience as a "parent educator" is limited. Is it presumptuous of me to undertake such a task? In answering this question, I reflected upon my long career as a psychologist and college professor and how I believe this has prepared me for the "task." I have had excellent training and extensive experience in a number of areas, including working with parents and children in individual and family therapy. I believe by providing information and insights from both a theoretical and clinical perspective, this book can become a very helpful resource for parents.

As previously noted, Dr. Robinson's work will be featured later in the book, hopefully in a way of which he would approve. Dr. Robinson and I shared a love of golf. He had a sign on his locker at his golf club, "Don't screw up." This was a line he used on many of his opponents which obviously can produce the opposite effect. Here I go – Joe. I hope I don't "screw it up."

Before presenting Dr. Robinson's approach to parenting, I believe it is important to review some of the more pertinent opinions regarding how to promote and encourage responsible behavior. As noted, Glasser's views will be presented as will those of selected others. Because of my family therapy training and bias, I will also present some basic information regarding child development, family structure and dynamics and healthy family functioning as well as an opportunity for you to explore certain aspects of your own family of origin.

As I further reflected on how I first came to learn of Dr. Robinson and his work, I became aware of how remarkable it was that teachers and other school professionals could readily identify his patients. What a legacy! I was able to interview several of the parents who worked with him. They all gave him a great deal of credit for their children's successes and for their own feelings of competency and satisfaction. One mother told me she gave him credit for how well her children handled her divorce. They told me of their children's accomplishments, and they all have continued to have positive ongoing relationships with their children and, in many cases, their children's spouses and children. To borrow a term from Murray Bowen, their children appeared to have achieved a high level of "individuation;" in other words, they knew how to take care of themselves and were comfortable in doing so while continuing to maintain emotional contact with their families of origin.

Dr. Robinson's former nurse told me how many of the parents openly expressed their respect and affection for him. She told me "the kids always came first" and the parents understood and accepted this. She said he could be very direct in communicating this to parents. He was somewhat authoritarian at times but only after he had established a good working relationships with parents. I know from my own relationship with him that he had a keen sense of humor. He told me it was important for parents to be able to laugh at themselves and to laugh with their children. He did not advocate a hostile sense of humor or humor that put down others. He discussed this with parents and would often present important information to parents in a humorous way if he felt they were going "off track" or getting a bit too serious.

Dr. Robinson maintained a remarkable career as a pediatrician and, more specifically, as a parent educator. I spoke with him about this several times. He was reluctant to accept much of the credit, telling me he felt it was his job to give parents help in raising their children. He said he wanted to give them their "money's worth." He was quick to give parents credit for any positive outcomes. He told me he was lucky to have so many responsible parents in his practice. He also told me he "fired" some parents who were unable or unwilling to follow his recommendations.

What was it about these parents that enabled them to benefit from Dr. Robinson's direction? I have attempted to answer that question in this book. I believe any serious discussion about childrearing obviously has to start with a focus on parents as individuals. What beliefs, attitudes, qualities and behaviors are needed for responsible parenting? I have addressed what I believe those to be. I obviously was not able to interview all of the parents who worked with Dr. Robinson. However, I am reasonably certain that their beliefs, attitudes, and behaviors were similar to those I am identifying and recommending.

I have found in working with parents that most were not fully aware of how profoundly they are influenced by their multigenerational families of origin in their parenting practices and in many other ways. With that in mind, this book focuses on families in some detail. Readers will also have the opportunity to explore many of their experiences in their families of origin by completing and reflecting on the results of the Family of Origin Survey (FOS).

I also believe it is important for parents to realize what is happening in terms of their children's emotional development. To that end I have included an overview of Erik Erickson's Theory of Psychosocial Development.

Most importantly, I have included some of Dr. Robinson's specific advice to parents. Unfortunately, it is not as complete as it would have been if he had been able to write this chapter. I hope that I have been able to include enough of his beliefs and advice to be helpful in your parenting. The latter sections of this book address some additional considerations and broader issues, including my very serious concerns about the negative consequences of overparenting.

Dr. Robinson referred to his work with parents and children as "Preventive Psychiatry." While he was not a trained psychiatrist, I believe this was a very accurate description of his work. He and I spoke numerous times about how any efforts at the primary prevention of emotional and behavioral problems had to include parent education. Throughout the book I will attempt to demonstrate that Dr. Robinson's approach was very consistent with what I consider to be sound psychological principles and theories. The sources that I have selected hopefully reflect this. Those same sources have been very helpful to me in my work with individuals and families.

If you do find the material in the book to be helpful for you as well, I suggest you keep it in a clearly visible and easily accessible place and refer to it frequently.

Dr. Robinson believed that if you are fortunate enough to become a parent, parenting must be one of the most important things in your life. I heartily agree. If you can accept that fact, the material in this book will have much greater meaning for you.

Dr. Robinson's basic parenting philosophy was one of "Judicious Neglect." He worked with parents to learn to trust the child's inner laws of development and to resist the temptation to "handle" the child excessively and to take them everywhere. He impressed upon them the fact that the child needed "alone time" to grow and develop in a healthy manner. He believed if parents learned to trust their baby's natural movement toward growth, children would be much more likely to naturally move toward healthy growth and development and parents would gain confidence in themselves and their parenting.

The phenomenon of overparenting is a current cause of concern for many mental health professionals, educators, and sociologists and will be addressed in some detail later in the book. Dr.

Robinson believed overparenting began in the very earliest stages of child-rearing. Since the goal of this book is to increase parents' sense of competency, the material was designed to be consistent with Dr. Robinson's philosophy and to help parents avoid the "overparenting trap."

The Robinson Way is not meant to represent the only way to raise children. However, the advice Dr. Robinson gave to parents was based on meticulous clinical research and obviously led to very positive results for his patients and their parents. Essentially Dr. Robinson strongly believed that children will, given the opportunity by their parents, grow and develop in response to the inner laws of development. Erik Erickson held similar beliefs regarding the child's emotional development. Dr. Robinson and I spoke several times regarding what he felt might happen to children who were over-parented. Current evidence would confirm many of our predicted outcomes.

Key Points

My Freshman Latin teacher, Sister Jeramine—all 4' 8" of her—impressed upon me both mentally and physically that, "Repetition is the mother of learning." I know that she was right because I still remember, among other things she taught me, the Latin cheer we used to learn how to conjugate verbs: "O or M, ST, Mustis, NT." This was repeated three times with increasing intensity and followed with a rousing, "Learn Latin thoroughly."

The Key Points that are included at the end of each chapter are repetitive by design, as are various other parts of this book. The laws of remembering and forgetting obviously apply to parenting as they do to other areas of our lives.

Dr. Robinson always spent some time communicating to parents the fact that parenting is a serious business and needs to be recognized as such. Not only are we significantly influencing the growth and development of our children but also that of their children and their children's children, as well as society in general.

As noted above, key points will be included at the end of each chapter along with some observations and ideas for using the material in the chapter. Picture Sister Jeramine on her much-needed raised platform leading the cheer, "Learn Responsible Parenting Thoroughly." Repetition is indeed the mother of learning and can lead to habit formation. A habit is simply something we do without thinking about it. Here's to establishing and practicing good parenting habits!

1

Responsibility, Discipline, Honesty, and Love

Raising responsible kids requires responsible parents. I have found that most of us who are fortunate to be parents consider ourselves to be responsible both as individuals and in our parenting. However, in working with parents, I found that many, even the most devoted, lacked a full understanding of the concept of responsibility and the importance of gaining this understanding. I have found similar confusion and uncertainty regarding the concepts of discipline and love in my discussions with individuals and parents. In this chapter I will address these concepts and discuss their crucial roles in achieving responsible parenting.

Responsibility

Webster's Collegiate Dictionary defines responsibility as the quality or state of being responsible. *Responsible* in turn is defined as being able to answer for one's conduct and obligations and being able to choose between right and wrong. As noted in the Introduction, responsibility is a core concept in Glasser's reality therapy. Dr.

Robinson also frequently used the term in discussing his work with parents and children. While he was not very familiar with Glasser's work, the similarities in his beliefs and those of Glasser were striking.

Glasser defines responsibility as "the ability to fulfill one's needs and to do so in a way that does not deprive others of the ability to fulfill their needs." The effective parent then needs to be responsible for their own need fulfillment while enabling and helping their children to learn the same. Glasser continues, "If we do not learn how to fulfill our needs, we will suffer all our lives; the younger and more thoroughly we learn, the more satisfactory our lives will be." Therefore, the process of "learning to fulfill our needs must begin early in infancy and continue all our lives." Dr. Robinson would heartily agree with these latter statements.

According to Glasser, we all have basically the same needs. What then are these needs? "First is the need to love and be loved." This need manifests itself in many ways throughout the life cycle but must begin with parental love or that of a surrogate caretaker. Glasser postulated other needs as well. "Equal in importance to the need for love is the need to feel we are worthwhile both to ourselves and to others. Although the two needs are separate, a person who is loved and can give love in return will usually feel that he is a worthwhile person and one who is worthwhile is usually someone who is loved and can give love in return." Glasser later proposed other needs, including the need to belong but to have a separate identity, the need for a sense of freedom and control, and, last but not least, the need for fun!

Need fulfillment always involves a firm emotional relationship with at least one other person. Glasser states, "the responsible parent creates the necessary involvement with his child and teaches him responsibility through the proper combination of love and discipline." He noted children will have difficulty accepting discipline unless they feel their parents care enough to actively show them responsible ways of living. He concluded, "we learn responsibility through involvements with responsible fellow human beings who will love and discipline us properly and who are intelligent enough to allow us freedom to try out our newly acquired responsibility as soon as we show readiness to do so."

Few parents would argue with having responsible children as a desirable goal and most realize that attaining this goal requires significant efforts on their part. However, many parents lack a full understanding of exactly what they are responsible for and, as a result, struggle with how best to fulfill these responsibilities.

Scott Peck in his brilliant and inspired work, *The Road Less Traveled* (which, by the way, was on the *New York Times* best seller list for over thirteen years), noted, "the problem of distinguishing what we are and what we are not responsible for in this life is one of the greatest problems of human existence." In Peck's opinion, it is a life-long challenge for us to discern on an ongoing basis where our priorities and responsibilities lie. Since we as individuals, families, and members of society go through various stages of development and changing circumstances, the problem in Peck's opinion is never completely solved. The need for this discernment of responsibilities is particularly crucial and difficult in the realm of parent-child relationships. It must begin with a thorough and honest self-evaluation of our attitudes and behaviors as parents. Peck pointed out that evaluating ourselves is not something we do instinctively or naturally. The process can be quite painful. It requires the courage to tolerate the resultant pain and the flexibility and self-discipline necessary to make whatever changes are necessary to accommodate the developmental needs of our children.

When we become parents, we do so in the context of all our various other responsibilities. The percentages of working mothers and single parents in our society have risen significantly in the last several decades. While there is a growing number of "Mr. Moms," most fathers also have to deal with the economic "sink or swim" realities. Fulfilling the demands of multiple roles and obligations further complicates the process of discerning responsibilities and priorities. Among these demands, our ongoing attachments and obligations including those within our family of origin must also be recognized, considered, and prioritized.

When two individuals choose to begin a family, they create what I like to call a living organism, which is referred to in systems theory as a spousal subsystem. When children enter the system, parental-child subsystems emerge. Children in turn can become part of one or more sibling subsystems. The demands of these subsystems can be quite diverse and even conflictual at times. As the family moves through the various developmental stages, accommodations and renegotiation of duties and boundaries must occur. Family members, parents, and children alike need to find ways to give in to the demands of the family system without giving up who they are.

Parents are, I believe, influenced significantly in their parenting on both a conscious and unconscious level by their experiences within their own multi-generational families of origin. The nuclear family needs to find a way to integrate and accommodate differences from maternal and paternal families of origin into a workable whole. Like all living organisms, the family system as a whole and the various subsystems need to be nurtured and attended to on an ongoing basis. Families as systems will be discussed in some detail in a later chapter.

Discipline

The reader will note that in parents' own lives and in helping to shape the direction of our children's lives, the need for discipline is paramount. Often when parents hear the word *discipline*, they think of harsh, overly strict, and sometimes punitive forms of discipline. This is not what is being advocated. That form of discipline is rarely effective in the long term. It is what Peck referred to as "undisciplined discipline."

Parents who engage in this form of discipline are undisciplined themselves. Often, "their own lives are frequently and obviously in disorder and disarray, and their attempts to order the lives of their children seem therefore to make little sense to these children." What kind of discipline is being recommended, and how is it achieved?

Peck addresses these questions in some detail. He believes that parents' primary responsibility is to teach their children how to solve problems, and the technique for solving problems is discipline. Peck tells us, "discipline is the basic set of tools we require in solving life's problems. Without discipline we can solve nothing. With only some discipline we can only solve some problems. With total discipline we can solve all problems." Effective problem-solving is the key to living a truly responsible life. However, confronting and solving problems also involves pain, and our natural response is to avoid pain. Failure to address and to try to resolve painful situations leads to a stunting of emotional and spiritual growth. If this pattern becomes habitual, it can lead to any number of emotional and behavioral disorders. At the very least, the tendency to deny and to fail to address problems will surely result in failure to reach one's full potential as a human being.

Peck continues, "let us teach ourselves and our children the necessity for suffering and the value thereof, the need to solve problems and to experience the pain involved." I have often told parents that all real growth (i.e. spiritual and emotional growth) is painful. If we can truly help our children learn to use discipline to solve their problems, they will be able to accept and tolerate the accompanying pain. Allowing children to solve their own problems when ready to do so requires parental restraint and that also can be painful. By providing appropriate discipline and modeling discipline in our own lives, we can also help our children achieve self-discipline. Achieving self-discipline is crucial before the onset of adolescence. Essentially, we have about a thirteen-year grace period to help our children learn self-discipline but as with most other things in life, the sooner the better.

What then are the tools of discipline? Peck lists the following four:

- delaying of gratification
- acceptance of responsibility
- dedication to truth
- balancing

Delaying Gratification

Peck noted, "delaying gratification is a process of scheduling the pain and pleasure of life in such a way to enhance the pleasure by meeting and experiencing the pain first and getting it over with. It is the only decent way to live." This principle was also clearly seen in "Grandma's law." Grandma insisted we ate our vegetables before we got our apple pie. Parenting presents countless opportunities to help our children learn how to delay gratification (e.g. homework or chores). Parents who have learned to do this in their own lives are much better able to take advantage of these opportunities and to provide positive role models for their children. Children who observe their parents behaving with self-discipline will come to believe, at the deepest level, that this is the right way to live.

Role modeling and teaching of discipline can only be truly effective if the child feels loved. As Glasser has noted, children will have difficulty accepting discipline unless they feel their parents care enough about them to actively show them responsible ways of behaving. Love provides the motivation to take the time to be fully with our children. This is best accomplished by being supportive but not overly intrusive. Only then can we understand their feelings and concerns and identify areas in which they need help in problem-solving. Effective problem-solving requires time as well as courage to address the problem. As noted above, the first step in learning to postpone gratification is: *Do the most difficult thing first.* This works particularly well with homework.

Acceptance of Responsibility

Before any problem can be solved, it must first be acknowledged. When we acknowledge a problem, we are in a position to accept responsibility for it. In the parlance of the day we can "own" it. This "owning" of the problem is necessary before we can determine how to solve it. If we see the problem as residing primarily within someone or something else, we will not find a real solution. Reality therapy is based on the assumption that everyone who is in need of psychological treatment has a common characteristic: "They all deny the reality of the world around them." Drug and Alcohol treatment programs stress the influence of denial in maintaining an addiction. A former colleague of mine who worked in a drug and alcohol treatment center frequently wore a tee shirt that said, "Denial is not a river in Egypt." Children by nature are likely to blame others for their difficulties. They need to actively be taught that while this acceptance of responsibility may bring short term pain, it is crucial to their emotional and spiritual growth and will ultimately pay great dividends.

Dedication to Truth

This obviously is closely related to the previous tool. When we accept reality, we are accepting truth, for they are interchangeable. Accepting truth may mean giving up long held or preconceived beliefs, notions, and attitudes and making revisions in our thinking. Again, this process can be quite painful and requires the courage to persist in spite of the pain. To have the discipline to do this, we must, in Peck's words, be totally dedicated to truth, and therefore lead a "life of continuous and never-ending stringent self-examination." As we accurately identify our reality, we need to simultaneously identify our own thoughts, beliefs, and behaviors.

If we choose to dedicate ourselves to truth, there are rules we must follow according to Peck. In addition to avoiding the obvious dishonesty that accompanies speaking falsehoods, Peck also considers withholding the truth to be potentially deceitful. The decision to do so "must always be based entirely upon the needs of the person from whom the truth is being withheld." However, in determining such a need, "the assessment of another's needs is an act of responsibility which is so complex that it can only be executed wisely when one operates with genuine love for the other." Peck cautions us that when assessing another's ability to accept the truth, there is a tendency to underestimate the individual's capacity of accepting and using the truth for their own spiritual or emotional growth.

This challenge of dedicating ourselves to truth requires never-ending self-discipline and a life of openness. While this is obviously very difficult, Peck tells us living this way can bring great rewards in all of our intimate relationships and can bring a true sense of freedom. Those who live this way are free to be themselves since they have nothing to hide. Peck notes if we choose to dedicate ourselves to truth, the energy required for honesty will be far less than that required for deception and secretiveness.

<u>Balancing</u>

Discipline is demanding and complex. Peck tells us it requires both flexibility and judgment. We can live a disciplined life and still be spontaneous. Remember Glasser's need for fun! Balancing gives us the flexibility to give in to the changing demands of living without giving up our basic integrity.

In parenting, as in other important areas of our lives, we "must daily delay gratification and keep an eye on the future; yet to live joyously we must also possess the capacity, when it is not destructive, to live in the present and act spontaneously." This kind of disciplined flexibility, which Peck referred to as "balancing," requires parents to learn to control their emotions and not allow their feelings to overwhelm their intellects while retaining the capacity to fully experience and appropriately express their emotions. This ability is part of what is now being referred to as "emotional intelligence," which will be discussed in a later chapter.

Peck notes that "mature mental health demands, then, an extraordinary capacity to strike and continually restrike a delicate balance between conflicting needs, goals, duties, responsibilities, directions, etc. The essence of this discipline of balance is 'giving up.'"

All giving up is painful, but without it we cannot grow. Just as we, at times, must give up long held beliefs, habits, and patterns of relating to others in order to grow, children also have to continually give up things as they go through the various developmental stages. The key for parents is to help their children do this when they are psychologically ready to do so. Determining this level of readiness requires close parental scrutiny of their children without undue intrusiveness.

Glasser and Peck tell us that responsible parenting involves a blending of discipline and love. Discipline enables parents and children to solve problems. The tools of discipline were presented and briefly discussed. I fully agree that we cannot be truly responsible as parents without discipline. If we want our children to grow to be responsible adults, we must help them to learn and continually practice the techniques of discipline. Spending time with our children and closely observing them is the only way to identify areas in which they need to improve their problem-solving abilities.

I have observed that many parents do a great deal *for* their children but not very much *with* them. Through our involvement we can also evaluate how truly helpful we are being. Being overly helpful may satisfy our needs, but it can be harmful when children have the ability and desire to help themselves. I have seen many examples of "help that hurts" in working with parents. As Glasser notes, we must find ways of fulfilling our needs without depriving our children of the ability to fulfill their needs. A common pattern for modern parents is to have their children become involved in a large number of structured activities and team sports. While this can be very helpful in many ways, watching them perform should not be seen as a total substitute for doing things with them.

Love

Very few parents need to be told to love their children. However, responsible parenting requires "responsible loving." Peck defines love as "the will to extend one's self for the purpose of nurturing one's own or another's spiritual growth." As can be seen in this definition, love is an active process often requiring a great deal of effort, and it involves loving both self and others.

We need to be concerned about our own spiritual growth or we cannot be truly concerned about the spiritual growth of another. In short, if we don't love ourselves, we really can't love another. Peck summarizes, "I therefore conclude that the desire to love is not itself love. Love is an act of will – namely, both an intention and action."

Peck feels we must not confuse this kind of love with romantic love or "falling in love." Falling in love is not something that we consciously choose to do, and falling in love is invariably temporary. No matter whom we fall in love with, we sooner or later fall out of love if the relationship continues long enough. To truly love ourselves and our children, spouses, siblings, parents on an ongoing basis in a way that promotes spiritual growth, we must continue to choose to do so, perhaps even on a day-to-day basis.

I have done a fair amount of marital therapy and have heard

spouses say that they have "fallen out of love." I can recall more than one wife stating that although her husband is a good person, provider, father, she just isn't "in love" with him anymore. This is not to say only women feel this way, but women are generally more able and likely to express themselves in therapy. For many marriages which end in a few years or less, the realization that their partner and marriage (and their children) are not perfect becomes the catalyst for divorce or separation. Since this is a book about parenting, I won't go into detail about marital problems. However, research and experience in family therapy points out that emotional problems in children are often closely related to unresolved marital conflicts.

Conclusion

Although the concepts of responsibility, discipline, honesty, and love were presented separately, they are clearly interrelated, and responsible parenting requires all to be seriously considered. Hopefully the information presented in this chapter will provide a deeper understanding of these concepts and perhaps some new perspectives on their meanings and role in the parenting process.

The issue of parental responsibility will be further discussed throughout this book. The specific needs of our children are rarely always the same as ours. I will stress the need for finding ways of entering the personal worlds of our children and learning their subjective perceptions and desires. As parents, it is easy to try too hard to force our children to live in our perceived world. Acts of parental over- or under-responsibility do not occur in a vacuum. Rather, they occur in numerous and varied contexts. Most significant among these contexts are our nuclear families and our multigenerational family of origin. As a helping professional, I believed it was important for me to understand these various contexts as fully as possible before attempting any interventions.

I briefly note some clinical examples of what would appear to be under- and over-responsible parenting in Chapter 3. While it would be easy to respond to these situations by blaming the parents for what would appear to be rather obvious poor judgment, I believe their actions can best be understood only when they are viewed as part of ongoing, dynamic family systems.

Key Points Chapter 1

Key Point #1

All of us, parents and children alike, are from the moment of birth striving to fulfill our needs. Very early in life we must for obvious reasons rely on others for need fulfillment. The challenge is to learn ways of fulfilling our needs on our own. As Glasser tells us, if we don't learn how to responsibly fulfill our needs, we will suffer in a number of ways throughout our lives. When we think of the process of parenting, the primary task may be described as helping our children learn how to fulfill their needs without violating the needs of others. In parenting groups, I have asked parents to brainstorm ideas for accomplishing this task. When done as couples, this has led to a number of impressive insights and ideas. In doing so it also has helped a number of parents to become more aware of their own needs and how, at times, they may conflict with the needs of their children.

Key Point #2

Scott Peck tells us that one of the greatest problems of human existence is figuring out what we are and are not responsible for in life. How can we help our children learn responsibility without hurting them in the process? As previously noted, I have frequently told parents that there is help that helps and help that hurts. Essentially, help that hurts occurs when we do something for our children that they are capable of—or almost capable of—doing for themselves. While this may make us feel better, our children have been deprived of an opportunity to develop a greater sense of competence, confidence, self-satisfaction, and responsibility.

Remember that the true discernment of responsibility is very difficult and ongoing. Many parents never successfully resolve this problem. I have worked with parents of adult children who struggled mightily in this regard. One of the exercises I have used in parent groups is to have both mother and father independently draw a line down the middle of a sheet of paper, listing on one side what they felt should be their primary responsibilities and listing their children's primary responsibilities on the other. Parents would then compare their worksheets and discuss similarities and differences. I believe it is imperative that any parental perceptions regarding responsibility that differ significantly need to be negotiated and hopefully resolved early on in the parenting process.

Key Point #3

Perhaps the greatest gift we can give our children is helping them learn self-discipline. As Peck tells us, discipline is the basic set of tools we use in solving life's problems. He notes that with total discipline we can solve all problems. Helping our children learn self-discipline is a process that can be difficult and painful for ourselves and our children. Far and away the most powerful way of helping our children learn self-discipline is by consistently displaying it in our own lives. Children from the start are very keen observers and they respond intuitively to what they are seeing and sensing emotionally. One of Dr. Robinson's basic instructions to parents was the need to model self-discipline for their children. He put it this way: "If you expect your kids to get their act together, then you have to get yours together." He emphasized the need for honesty and integrity (which he defined as keeping our promises) in our dealings with our children and others. Remember they are watching and learning.

Peck describes in detail the importance of dedicating ourselves to the truth. I frequently have asked parents to evaluate their own behaviors and their interactions with their children using Peck's "tools" of discipline as a guideline.

Key Point #4

Glasser and Peck stress the need for both love and discipline in parenting. Finding the right combination of love and discipline can be difficult. Glasser tells us of the importance of the need to love and be loved, and Peck stresses the need for discipline to solve life's problems. Love is seen as the will to act in ways that nurture spiritual growth, both our own and that of our children. Remember love is a choice rather than just a feeling. One of my favorite parenting group exercises was to have parents evaluate the ways in which they demonstrate love for their children (using Peck's definition). With some practice, they could identify those manifestations of love that were more likely to foster their children's spiritual growth and those that might hinder their spiritual growth. I would point out that ultimately, as our children grow and mature, the only real connection we have with them is the relationship we establish and maintain during childrearing. I have found the kind of love that nurtures spiritual growth and development to be both lasting and fulfilling.

Works Cited

Glasser, W. (1965). *Reality therapy*. New York, NY: Harper & Row.
Peck, M. S. (1978). *The road less traveled*. New York, NY: Simon & Schuster.

2

Intelligent Parenting

Considering the enormous challenge of being a responsible parent, obviously the more cognitive ability we can apply to the task, the greater the potential for success. First and foremost, we need to fully conceptualize the great privilege and responsibility we have been given in helping to shape the growth and development of another human being. In addition, we need to realize we will be called upon to make countless decisions regarding the best interests of our children. A single decision regarding their health, education, or overall welfare can have very significant consequences for their long-term well-being.

Unfortunately, unlike the children of Garrison Keillor's "Lake Wobegon," we can't all be above average intellectually. As a psychologist I can say with a good deal of certainty that intelligence is normally distributed among any given population. Like it or not, 68.26% of us will be within plus or minus one standard deviation of the mean. The good news is we don't have to be gifted intellectually to continue learning throughout our lives or to be good parents. If we choose to, we can find numerous ways to become more and more knowledgeable as individuals and parents.

While intelligence *can* be a great asset to parents, this is not always the case. Many of the very brightest people struggle greatly as parents. Some fail almost completely at the task. Conversely, others with more modest native endowments and less formal education are excellent parents. Intellectual ability does not in itself appear to be the "common denominator" of effective parenting.

Recent research in neuroanatomy clearly demonstrates that the emotional centers in our brain can strongly influence and at times dominate the thinking centers. Daniel Goleman in *Emotional Intelligence*, an excellent discussion of this topic, noted that in addition to cognitive ability, another kind of intelligence, "emotional intelligence," is needed to effectively manage the complexities of life. Few situations are more complex than parent-child relationships. He described emotional intelligence as including characteristics such as, "being able to motivate oneself and persist in the face of frustration; to control impulses and delay gratification; to regulate one's moods and keep distress from swamping the ability to think; to empathize and to hope."

Salovey and Mayer offered an elaborated definition of emotional intelligence which divided it into five domains:

- *"Knowing one's emotions:* Self-awareness—recognizing a feeling as it happens—is the keystone of emotional intelligence.
- *Managing Emotions:* Handling feelings so they are appropriate is an ability that builds on self-awareness.
- *Motivating oneself:* […] Emotional self-control, delaying gratification and stifling impulsiveness underlies accomplishments of every sort.
- *Recognizing emotions in others:* Empathy, another ability that builds on self-awareness, is the fundamental people skill.
- *Handling relationships:* The art of relationships is, in large part, skill in managing others."

Goleman likewise asserts, "No one can yet say exactly how much of the variability from person to person in life's course it [emotional intelligence] accounts for. But what data exist suggests it can be as powerful and at times more powerful than IQ." These crucial emotional competencies can be learned and improved upon throughout life. However, they are best learned in childhood. We can help ourselves and our children to develop these competencies in a number of ways.

Empathy

Of all of the abilities comprising emotional intelligence, perhaps the most crucial in parenting is empathy. Empathetic understanding is an invaluable skill in many contexts. For example, successful therapeutic relationships are based on empathetic understanding. Since I believe what happens in therapy closely resembles what happens (or should happen) in parenting, the potential advantages are obvious.

I believe it is important to distinguish between empathy and sympathy. Sympathy is essentially something we feel *for* someone while empathy involves feeling *with* someone. That is, experiencing what someone is feeling or experiencing *as if* it were happening to you. However, it is important not to lose the "as if" quality. If we do, we may become as upset or confused as the other person if there is a serious problem or conflict.

One of my early therapy supervisors was a psychiatrist by the name of Louis Vitale. Dr. Vitale and I met each week to review my cases. He always cautioned me when he sensed I may be feeling sorry for a client. His concern was that if that happened, I would not expect the client to help themselves. While it is natural to feel compassion for someone with problems, we need, at times, to be able to distance ourselves from these feelings in order to accurately empathize and help that person toward resolution of their problems. Dr. Vitale's supervision was extremely helpful to me both as a professional and as a parent.

In my university career, I was responsible for training counselors and therapists. I was always struck by the differences in students' ability to empathize. I felt there may be a genetic predisposition to learn to truly experience and understand another's feelings. Despite a variety of training exercises, practica, and internships, some individuals continued to struggle with becoming more empathetic. I am unaware of any research supporting a genetic link, but there are studies indicating that the way we were raised strongly influences our ability to be empathetic.

Recent research into the concept of empathy has shown that the roots of empathy begin in infancy and that children show differences at a very early age. Goleman cites a series of studies at the National Institute of Mental Health which showed a large part of the difference in empathetic concern had to do with how parents disciplined their children. Children were more empathetic when the discipline included calling strong attention to the distress their misbehavior caused someone else. Further, "they found too that children's empathy is also shaped by [...] imitating what they see." If parents can clearly demonstrate sensitivity in their ongoing interactions, children will be more likely to respond empathically to others. Goleman also points out, "Empathy builds on self-awareness; the more open we are to our own emotions, the more skilled we will be in reading feelings." While it might seem cliché to say that it is important for parents to get in touch with their feelings, many of us grew up in families that did not encourage or perhaps even allow for the open expression of feelings. Having done my share of marital therapy, I can state that lack of recognition and expression of feelings has often been a significant underlying part of many marital and family problems.

It is also important to realize that accurate empathy requires being able to read and interpret nonverbal as well as verbal communication. Goleman cites a large-scale study conducted by Robert Rosenthal, a Harvard psychologist: "In tests with over seven thousand people in the U.S. and eighteen other countries, the benefits of being able to read feelings from nonverbal cues included being better adjusted emotionally, more popular, more outgoing and perhaps not surprisingly—more sensitive." Since females are generally better than males in responding to nonverbal cues, I have at times encouraged wives to work with husbands to increase their skills in this area, hopefully in a gentle, non-judgmental way. Perhaps a friendly game or two of charades would be helpful. Goleman points out, "Empathy requires enough calm and receptivity so that the subtle signs of feeling from another person can be received and mimicked by one's emotional brain."

Dr. Daniel Stern, a psychiatrist, refers to moments of empathy between parent and child as "attunement." These attunements begin in infancy and, ideally, continue throughout life. Goleman noted, "Prolonged absence of attunement between parent and child takes a tremendous toll on the child. When a parent consistently fails to show any empathy with a particular range of emotions in the child—joy, tears, needing to cuddle—the child begins to avoid expressing and perhaps even feeling those same emotions."

The Amygdala

One of my standard pieces of advice to clients over the years has been to try very hard not to say or do what they feel like saying or doing when they are emotionally upset. In particular, I told parents that what they felt like saying or doing when they were very upset would almost always be the wrong thing. Responding emotionally at times of intense conflict is very likely to feed into a "conflict cycle" with our children and rarely leads to any viable solutions. In addition, acting on emotion at times of high arousal can be very damaging to a child's emerging sense of self and could lead to ongoing communication and relationship problems. *"Somebody has to be the adult,*" way the way I would put it. While I knew experientially that I was giving sound advice, there is now scientific validation.

Goleman cites the work of Joseph Le Doux, a neuroscientist who was the first to discover the key role that an almond-shaped cluster of interconnected structures within the brain, called the amygdala, plays as a store house of emotional memory and a kind of "emotional sentinel." Goleman describes, "When it sounds an alarm of fear it sends urgent messages to every major part of the brain; it triggers the secretion of the body's hormones, mobilizes the centers for movement, and activates the cardiovascular system, the muscles and the gut." While this activation of the fight or flight response system can be of crucial importance in some emergency situations, it is rarely helpful in resolving interpersonal conflicts. Basically, when we overreact emotionally, we have been "hijacked" by our amygdala.

Goleman further explains, "Le Doux's research explains how the amygdala can take control over what we do even as the thinking brain, the neocortex, is still coming to a decision." In short, no matter how intelligent or knowledgeable we may be as parents we still can make critical mistakes in dealing with our children when our emotions overtake our intellect. Moreover, this process of "emotional hijacking" takes place in milliseconds and remains stored in our emotional working memory. Essentially, "the more intense the emotional arousal, the stronger the imprint; the experiences that scare or thrill us the most are our most indelible memories." In simple terms, this research points out that the brain has two separate memory systems, one for factual data and one for emotional memories.

Goleman explains, "A special system for emotional memories makes excellent sense in evolution, of course, insuring that animals would have particularly vivid memories of what threatens or pleases them. But emotional memories can be faulty guides to the present." In other words, the emotional mind, which responds much more quickly at times of high intensity than the thinking part of the brain, may sacrifice accuracy for speed and make critical errors. If certain emotional components of the current situation resemble a previous situation, our response may be fast but inappropriate to the situation at hand. In order to consistently function effectively as parents, we need to be able to identify when we feel we are beginning to lose emotional control and develop ways of responding that do not feed into a conflict cycle with our children. I'm sure all of us have seen how a relatively minor incident can escalate into an out of control situation once the emotions overtake the intellect.

I am reminded of a family I worked with whose oldest child was a very bright, very assertive adolescent girl. She had long since learned how to manipulate her mother. Her father, who had been largely on the periphery of the family system, was now entering the fray. When her father refused a request, she would respond by telling him how much she hated him and how she wished she had another father. His response to this was essentially to "lose it" and their encounters were becoming more and more intense to the point of being potentially dangerous.

In a separate session with "Dad," I first helped him identify the subtle physiological cues that signaled his "neural alarm" was about to go off. I had earlier helped him learn and practice diaphragmatic breathing. When he felt the tension begin to build in the back of his neck, he would focus on his breathing and was less likely to be emotionally reactive. But he still needed a default response to his daughter's verbal attacks. We decided on a "broken record" response that always began with "I can see that you're upset" followed by his rational response to her requests, always in a calm tone of voice. His daughter didn't appreciate the broken record response, but she recognized that while he was being somewhat empathetic, he wasn't likely to change his mind and, more importantly, was not going to lose control of his emotions.

Over a relatively short period of time, their encounters became much less contentious and their overall communication improved considerably. By not responding in kind to his daughter's attacks, he broke the conflict cycle. We later were able to identify the reasons underlying the father's emotional overreacting which, not surprisingly, came primarily from his family of origin. However, he had to remain vigilant to control his responses to emotionally charged encounters with his daughter.

There is also a second kind of emotional reaction, slower than the quick response, which simmers and brews first in our thoughts before it leads to feeling. This is the cornerstone of cognitive therapy, first introduced by Albert Ellis as Rational Emotional Therapy. In this approach, clients learn that essentially what we tell ourselves about a certain situation determines our emotional response to it. If we can identify any irrational or unhelpful cognitions (in our self-talk) which may be causing emotional distress or inappropriate responses, we can begin to challenge and change them and hopefully gain better control over our emotional responses.

Many of our thoughts about parenting and our appraisals of relevant situations as parents—what Ellis would call irrational—can and do cause excessive anxiety, fear, anger, and resentment. The "shoulds," "musts," and "ought to's" associated with parenting can be particularly harmful. For example, children "should" always listen to their parents, "must" always agree with them, and "ought to" always treat them with respect, even when upset. And of course, parents "always" know best. This kind of thinking can significantly limit our ability to function effectively. We need to develop the self-awareness necessary to identify these faulty cognitions and find ways of changing them. Can you see how these may lead to stress, anxiety, anger, and excessive worrying which in turn can lead to distress and a lack of effectiveness as parents? We need to ask what the consequences of these actions, thoughts, and resultant feelings are for us and those we care about. We need to remember that the rational mind does not act as rapidly as the emotional mind. When we develop a reasonable understanding of what it is we are thinking and feeling, we can begin to gain more control over our behavior and its consequences and later examine the "why" of our thoughts and feelings.

Remember that when a present situation is experienced as similar to an emotionally charged past event, the emotional mind will react as if the past event were occurring now. This is clear to see in fearful or threatening events. A good example of this is the mental disorder known as Posttraumatic Stress Disorder or PTSD. In this disorder the patient feels the same intense fear, horror, or helplessness that was felt at the time of the traumatic event. If untreated, this can lead to a number of severe symptoms of mental distress.

I am reminded of the case of a young woman with whom I had been working a number of years ago. She had been a nurse in a psychiatric hospital. When walking through a ward she was attacked from behind by a very strong female patient. She suffered a number of physical injuries and had to give up her nursing career. At a therapy session with me, she related the following incident. She was shopping at a mall with her husband, but they had gone their separate ways within the mall. She was walking toward a store when she suddenly froze and was unable to move, shout, or ask for help. She stood motionless for some time until her husband saw her and was able to help her. When she and I discussed this, she remembered that she heard some footsteps coming up behind her and she felt intense fear and anxiety. The emotional intensity of the original trauma returned and paralyzed her. Fortunately, she responded quite well to therapy and gradually became much less reactive to potential "triggers" which could emotionally recreate the original trauma.

In addition to these traumatic or very intense situations we can also be influenced strongly by less obvious emotional reactions. Goleman suggests, "if the feelings are vague or subtle, we may not quite realize the emotional reaction we are having even though it is subtly coloring how we may react to the moment. Thoughts and reactions at this moment will take on the coloration of thoughts and reactions then, even though it may seem that the reaction is due solely to the circumstance of the moment." Essentially, we really have no idea of what is going on, but we give ourselves a logical explanation for it; "at such moments the emotional mind has entrained the rational mind, putting it to its own uses."

I have found that the real or perceived faults we see in our children that upset us the most are those that remind us of our own or our spouses' faults. While children will act in ways that are indeed similar to us, we need to frequently remind ourselves that our children are unique individuals in their own right. Doing so will minimize the likelihood of responding emotionally rather than rationally to any "faults" or negative behaviors.

It is my contention that many of the emotional memories that have the potential to "hijack" us as parents come from within our multigenerational families of origin. I am not here endorsing a rather common current belief system that says we are all genetically or environmentally predetermined and unable to rise above these influences. Blaming our parents or grandparents for our current problems, even if somewhat deserved, can and often does lead to self-pity and pessimism which intensify rather than help find solutions to our problems. As previously noted, I will share many of my observations and feelings about families in a later chapter.

Goleman, Boyatzis, and McKeen in their book *Primal Leadership* broke emotional intelligence skills into four categories: Self-Awareness, Self-Management, Social Awareness and Relationship Management. The first two focus primarily on ourselves, while the latter two focus primarily on how we interact with others, including our children. Previously noted skills such as being able to motivate ourselves and persist in the face of frustration, controlling our impulses, delaying gratification, regulating our moods, maintaining optimism, and keeping distress from swamping our ability to think rationally are clear examples of personal emotional intelligence. As Peck noted, developing and using these skills is not possible without self-awareness and an honest, thorough self-evaluation. Since I firmly believe that responsible living and parenting are internally rather than externally controlled processes, the importance of the skills of self-awareness and self-management cannot be overstated.

Social awareness is obviously crucial to understanding others and requires, above all, the ability and willingness to empathize and focus on what others are feeling and do so in a non-judgmental way. This can enable us to establish and maintain lasting and satisfying relationships and accomplish interpersonal goals. Having a high level of social skill does not give us license to manipulate and control others for our personal goals. However, by using the skills of self-awareness, self-management, and social awareness in a principled way, we can become increasingly successful in our communications and particularly in resolving any conflicts that may occur in our significant interpersonal relationships, including our parenting.

Up to this point my presentation of the "responsible" and "intelligent" parent no doubt may seem a bit idealistic. It is not my intent to suggest that parents have to be perfect in order to be effective. Thomas Gordon, a psychologist who developed "Parent Effectiveness Training," noted, "parents are persons, not gods." Expecting ourselves or our parenting partners to be perfect can be detrimental to our success and lead to a number of irrational thoughts, expectations, and undue harsh self-criticism. However, it is my hope that some of the information presented thus far can help parents to better appreciate the complexity and inherent difficulties of the parenting process as well as the need for self-awareness and monitoring of their emotional responses in their interactions with their children. Excessive striving for perfectionism in self or others is always counterproductive. It is important to accept that we will, for a variety of reasons and despite our best intentions, make mistakes as parents. Accepting this fact can help to reduce the guilt which so many parents experience.

Goleman cites recent research "showing that having emotionally intelligent parents is itself of enormous benefit to a child." Children are astute observers of the way we relate to our partners emotionally as well as to them and therefore learn lessons that can be crucially important in developing emotional intelligence. Goleman points to research conducted at the University of Washington which found that "couples who were more emotionally competent in their marriage were also the most effective in helping their children with their emotional ups and downs." The research teams, led by Carole Hooven and John Gottman, were able to identify what they referred to as the parent's emotional style. They identified "emotionally inept" parenting styles. Below are descriptions of the three most commonly observed emotionally inept styles:

- *"Ignoring feelings altogether.* Such parents treat a child's emotional upset as trivial or a bother, something they should wait to blow over. They fail to use emotional moments as a chance to get closer to the child or to help the child learn lessons in emotional competence.
- *Being too laissez-faire.* These parents notice how a child feels but hold that however a child handles the emotional storm is fine—even, say hitting. Like those who ignore a child's feelings, these parents rarely step in to show their child an alternative emotional response. They try to soothe all upsets and will for instance, use bargaining and bribes to get their child to stop being sad or angry.
- *Being contemptuous, showing no respect for how the child feels.* Such parents are typically disapproving, harsh in both their criticisms and their punishments. They might, for instance, forbid any display of the child's anger at all, and become punitive at the least sign of irritability. There are the parents who angrily yell at a child who is trying to tell his side of the story, 'Don't you talk back to me!'"

Importantly, the researchers identified a successful parenting style that recognized "the opportunity of a child's upset to act as what amounts to as an emotional coach or mentor. They take their child's feelings seriously enough to try to understand exactly what is upsetting them…and to help the child find positive ways to soothe their feelings." Obviously, in order to effectively function as an emotional mentor or coach, parents must have a fairly good grasp of what constitutes emotional intelligence themselves.

In addition to controlling our own emotional responses, both as individuals and as spouses, I believe parents have a responsibility to facilitate and nurture their children's emotional development and help them become more emotionally competent. One of the more effective ways of fulfilling this responsibility is by understanding the importance of emotional intelligence and modeling it in our own lives.

Key Points Chapter 2

Key Point #1

Remember there is a good deal of scientific evidence indicating that our emotional responses to our children can have significant and lasting consequences for their emotional well-being. We need to take our children's feelings seriously, particularly when they are upset. By responding appropriately, we can serve as emotional coaches or mentors and help them learn emotional intelligence. Another powerful way of helping our children develop emotional intelligence is by demonstrating it in our relationships with others, including other family members and particularly our spouses.

Key Point #2

The brain does indeed have two memory systems, but our emotional memories can be faulty guides to present situations. As individuals and as parents we need to become vigilant in identifying potential triggers of our neural alarms and work to control the responses to the triggers. Since the Amygdala can activate emotional centers of the brain in milliseconds, we often won't have time to think through our responses. I have worked with parents to help them anticipate and practice alternative responses. In responding it is imperative that we do not do anything that seriously impairs our relationships with our children or parenting partners. Remember, too, that by showing patience and restraint in our responses at times of emotional arousal, we are serving as powerful models of emotional intelligence for our children.

Key Point #3

Of all of the various components of emotional intelligence, perhaps empathy is the most crucial. Understanding the need for empathy and developing our ability to respond empathetically will greatly enhance our relationships with our children and our effectiveness as parents.

Key Point #4

Irrational beliefs and negative self-talk can often be the cause of emotional distress. As individuals and particularly as parents, we need to identify faulty cognitions and work and practice to challenge and change them.

Key Point #5

No matter how bright or well educated we are, there are times when our emotions may overwhelm our intellects and cause us to be emotionally "hijacked." When this happens, it should be seen as a powerful learning experience. As Thomas Gordon tells us, "parents are persons, not gods." We need to forgive ourselves, learn from our mistakes, and continue to strive for higher levels of emotional intelligence.

Works Cited

Goleman, D. (1995). *Emotional intelligence.* New York, NY: Bantam Books.

Goleman, D., Boyatzis, R., McKee, A. (2013). *Primal leadership: Unleashing the power of emotional intelligence.* Boston, MA: Harvard Business Review Press.

Gordon, T. (2000). *Parent effectiveness training: The proven program for raising responsible children.* New York, NY: Three Rivers Press.

Hooven, C. & Gottman, J. as cited in Goleman, D. (1995). Emotional intelligence. New York, NY: Bantam Books.

Le Doux, J. as cited in Goleman, D. (1995). *Emotional intelligence.* New York, NY: Bantam Books.

Salovey, P. & Mayer, J. as cited in Goleman, D. (1995). *Emotional intelligence.* New York, NY: Bantam Books.

Stern, D. as cited in Goleman, D. (1995). *Emotional intelligence.* New York, NY: Bantam Books.

3

It's (Almost) All in the Family

Up to this point, I have attempted to offer some insights and information which I believe will be helpful to parents. However, I fully understand that to act with true responsibility, self-discipline, and emotional intelligence is easier said than done. This is where I feel many other books about parenting fall short. Merely knowing what to do is not enough. Many of us after reading a helpful book or attending a workshop try to follow the advice given and institute changes in our behavior. However, once the enthusiasm or momentum subsides, we may find ourselves falling into old, less effective patterns of behavior. This is especially true when, as in parenting, we are attempting to change our own behavior and influence the behavior of others.

I believe consistently responsible parenting is most likely to occur in a functional family system. How can we tell if our family system is functional? In order to assess the functionality of our family, we need to learn how to "think systems;" that is, examining and understanding the behaviors of family members, including our own, from an interactional perspective. We do not need to formally study systems theory, but we need to develop an awareness of how strongly our behaviors are influenced by the context in which they occur.

I believe that many of the efforts at educating parents fall short of the mark because parent-child relationships are often seen as isolated incidents rather than influenced in large measure by the context in which they occur. In a culture that rewards and encourages individual autonomy it is easy to lose sight of ourselves as interdependently tied to a larger system or systems. However, I believe we need to understand and accept this and become aware of how powerfully we are influenced as individuals and family members by the interactional processes both within our nuclear families and our multigenerational families of origin.

I was very fortunate to have participated in family therapy training at the Philadelphia Child Guidance Clinic, which has been for some time one of the leading centers in the family therapy field. This training enabled me to look at problems in a whole new light. I was able to see problems not as residing solely within individuals but within the larger system as well. By "thinking systems," I was able to gain a much clearer understanding of how problems not only develop but how they can be maintained by the family system and, how at times, they serve a role in maintaining family stability. As a result, I was also able to identify many additional points of intervention in order to help bring about change within a family. I had to learn to "think systems" in order to be effective. I believe as parents we also need to learn how to "think systems." Before we can begin thinking this way, I believe we need to learn a bit about systems as seen from theoretical and therapeutic viewpoints.

General systems theory (GST) was developed by a German biologist, Ludwig von Bertalanffy. He defined a system as "any entity maintained by the mutual interaction of its parts. A system can be composed of smaller systems and can be part of a larger system [...] Consequently, the same organized entity can be regarded as either a system or a subsystem depending on the observer's focus of interest." Therefore, we can think of our nuclear family (parents/parent and children) as composed of several subsystems and also as a subsystem within the parents/parent family/families of origin as well as within the larger ecosystem. The key concept is that all of these systems *are maintained by the mutual interaction of their parts.* To change the system and the resultant behaviors of those within the system we need to change the interactional patterns. Once these patterns become well established, we refer to them as transactional. Unfortunately, transactional patterns are highly resistant to change.

As a family therapist I saw my role as focusing upon these transactional patterns rather than on the individual characteristics of family members. By helping parents to more closely observe and identify interactions that may be maintaining problematic behaviors, we could discover potential ways of changing those patterns of interaction. Ultimately, this proved to be much more productive than trying to change individuals. I have observed many parents expending a great deal of energy trying to change their children rather than carefully examining and perhaps changing the patterns of their interactions with them.

I believe there are several concepts derived from systems theory and family therapy that have been helpful to me and that I believe may be helpful for parents to be aware of and understand in order to begin to "think systems."

1. **Nonsummativity**. This refers to the fact that a system is more than the sum total of its parts. Bertalanffy noted that a system is more than the sum of its parts just as a watch or a car is more than just a collection of parts. He noted that when things are organized in a pattern – a wholeness emerges out of that pattern. A family system then is more than just a collection of individuals. Hopefully, family members experience a sense of togetherness, a secure attachment and a sense of "having each other's backs." Once we become a family with an organized pattern of interactions, we develop a unified identity, a sense of "we-ness." We are no longer Mr. & Mrs. Jones and their children; we become the "Jones.'" Consciously and

unconsciously, family members make a commitment to attempt to try to meet each other's needs as well as the needs of the overall system. The psychologist, Urie Brofenbrenner, described families as groups of individuals *irrationally* committed to meeting each other's needs. I believe this is very accurate. The problem is, at times, these "irrational" actions or beliefs might not be in the best interest of family members.

2. **Equifinality**. This concept tells us that systems (families) begin at different starting points and they can and do find a number of different ways of reaching their goal. While perhaps not all roads lead to "Rome," many roads do. As human beings, we are by nature creative and spontaneous and these characteristics, if utilized, can help us to achieve our goals. We need to be alert and open to all of the potential resources within and outside of the system which can be utilized in goal attainment and problem resolution. Many non-traditional and unconventional families function quite well.

3. **Homeostasis**. This concept tells us that systems strive to maintain a constant level of functioning in response to demands for change from within or outside of the system. Much like a thermostat or other self-regulating device, there are mechanisms within family systems designed to maintain the status quo. While these seemingly automatic mechanisms can be quite helpful, they can also make systems (families) highly resistant to change. Challenging or attempting to change the status quo may be disruptive but is sometimes necessary. A frequent observation in family therapy is that when the identified patient becomes better, this can upset the family's homeostatic balance and some other family member becomes symptomatic.

4. **Feedback Loops**. Within any system there are negative "feedback loops" that can reduce deviation to change and positive feedback loops that amplify change. It is important to identify these feedback

processes and their impact upon the overall system and individuals within the system. Who talks to whom and in what manner? How are these messages received? How do family members not directly involved in the communication respond?

5. **Rules**. All systems in order to achieve their goals and maintain order need rules. As parents it is important to establish and enforce rules. Systems have both explicit and implicit rules which need to be understood and communicated by parents to their children if order is to be maintained. Having clearly defined rules and taking the time to actively enforce these rules can be extremely helpful.

When I consulted with elementary school teachers, I would always ask them to formulate a list of rules if they had not already done so. Kids can be involved in helping to come up with what's appropriate for the list. Once formulated, I suggested they post the rules in conspicuous places and go over the rules at the beginning of each school day until the teacher was convinced they had been "overlearned." Once established, teachers could use the trick of "catching" the child following the rules. As parents, paying attention to children when they are behaving appropriately and not just when they are misbehaving can be a powerful reinforcer of good behavior.

6. **Power Hierarchies**. Functional systems require a clearly defined power hierarchy. Parents, like it or not, need to be in charge. Obviously, they can, when appropriate, delegate some of this power and authority to children. Even though we live in a democratic society, trying to have totally democratic families simply doesn't work.

7. **Values**. All functional systems have values which influence and direct activity within and outside of the system. It is very important, in my opinion, for parents to clarify their own values and those to which they would like their children to aspire.

8. **Boundaries**. In systems theory the family is viewed as "an organism, an open system, made up of subsystems each of which is surrounded by a semipermeable boundary, which is really a set of rules governing who is included within that subsystem and how they interact with those inside and outside it." Appropriate establishment and maintenance of boundaries both around the system as a whole and around the various subsystems is crucial to healthy family functioning. Boundaries will be discussed in greater detail later in this chapter.

9. **Circular Causality**. This is a key concept in Systems Theory and challenges the Newtonian view of causality (i.e. linear causality). In linear causality, A causes B, as in a parent causes a child's poor behavior. Circular causality would see the behavior as maintained by circular feedback loops or patterns of interactions between the parent and child and/or other family members rather than exclusively caused by the actions of either the parent or the child.

10. **Individuation/ Differentiation**. This concept, developed primarily by Murray Bowen, sees the goal of family systems as helping children individuate and learn how to function independently. To do so they must differentiate themselves from certain aspects of the family system without cutting off emotionally from their parents or other family members. If parents did not sufficiently differentiate from their families of origin, this will be carried over into their nuclear families. Bowen referred to this as the multigenerational transmission process which may adversely affect children within the nuclear family's ability to individuate in their own right. Bowen's theory will be discussed is more detail later in this chapter.

I previously noted the potential advantages to parents of "thinking systems." When we think systems, we direct our attention away from individuals within the system and examine the interactional processes and relationship issues. We can begin to think in terms of mutual interactions and circular rather than linear (A causes B) causality. In my work with families this was an important, if somewhat difficult to attain, first step toward problem resolution. For example, in a family where mother is openly critical of her husband's ineffectiveness as a parent, we need to look closely at how she is delivering this message and what are the reactions of the father and other members of the system. Are her attempts at motivating him having a positive effect, or are they resulting in him being less effective? It is important to look at the dynamics of the communication as well as the content of the message. These may be multiple reasons if mother's messages are rather harsh and critical. Before these can be explored, I would encourage mother to try a different approach to obtaining father's support and help as a parent. Since the marital and parental subsystems both require mutual respect and complementarity, each parent may have to give up part of their separateness in order to attain mutual interdependence. One of my goals in marital and family therapy was to help couples move toward symmetrical patterns of interaction both as husband and wife and as parents. Dependent/counter dependent relationships may help to establish relationships early on, but they are much less effective in the long run, particularly in parenting.

To go back to our hypothetical family, if I can get mother to see that her requests for help are ineffective, I can ask her to try another way of asking for help. As a result, the blame for not having father become a "better" parent is now placed on the communication rather than the individuals. Nobody's at fault from a circular cause and effect perspective. It is important to remember that mother and father are also husband and wife. Although these subsystems have somewhat differing roles and responsibilities at times, communication problems will adversely affect both. One of the standard complaints in couples/family therapy is, "They just don't listen to me." My response would be, "You need to find a way of talking to them so that they will listen," thereby placing responsibility on both the sender and receiver of the message. Simple interventions such as this done in the session with my coaching can bring significant changes. A former Philosophy professor of mine would frequently use the expression "Mutis Mutandi." Loosely translated – Change begets change. Remember that systems, particularly family systems, are highly resistant to change. Once change occurs, no matter how small, the potential for further changes is significantly enhanced.

As previously stated, I believe responsible parenting is most likely to consistently occur in a functional family system. There is no perfect family system just as there are no perfect parents. We can, theoretically at least, consider a continuum of family systems ranging from highly functional to highly dysfunctional. Functional families have clearly defined roles and responsibilities, clear and permeable boundaries, particularly generational boundaries and effective methods of communication. I have found one of the most viable theoretical models for assessing family systems functionality to be structural family therapy (SFT). This approach holds that all families have a structure which is only revealed when we look at the dynamic interactions of that family. Particular importance in this approach is placed upon the boundaries around and within the system. As stated above, boundaries need to be clear and permeable as opposed to overly rigid or diffuse.

If the family's boundaries are too open or diffuse this can lead to family members becoming too enmeshed with each other. When this happens anxiety can move too rapidly from one person to another and independent behavior cannot occur. Even the simplest problem can become a crisis. If, on the other hand, the boundaries are too rigid or closed, family members cannot respond appropriately to each other's emotional needs except perhaps in a crisis. Families with boundaries that are either too diffuse or too rigid cannot allow for appropriate adaptation to external stressors or demands for developmental changes within the family system.

Salvador Minuchin, the leading proponent of SFT, in *Families and Family Therapy*, proposes a continuum of boundary setting ranging from what he refers to as "disengaged" to "enmeshed." As noted above, research in family therapy indicates that families with clear and permeable boundaries, rather than disengaged or enmeshed boundaries have the flexibility to respond more appropriately to the developmental demands of the system and are much more effective in problem solving. From a boundary setting and communication perspective, these families are much more likely to consistently maintain functional patterns of behavior.

As previously noted, the units by which families carry out their functions are called subsystems. Subsystems can also be assessed in terms of functionality. In order to consistently accomplish required tasks, boundaries around each subsystem also need to be clear and permeable but not overly rigid or diffuse. I believe it is particularly crucial in families to maintain generational boundaries. I've noticed many "modern" families whose organizational patterns allow for children to have "total access" to their parents.

An example, in my opinion, of a lack of generational boundaries appeared on the cover of *Time* magazine's May 21, 2012 edition. A mother was pictured breast feeding her three-year-old son. She is a follower of the teachings of a pediatrician by the name of Dr. William Sears, author of the *Baby Book*. Sears advocates what he calls "attachment parenting." The three basic tenets according to *Time* are: "breast-feeding (sometimes into toddlerhood)," co-sleeping (inviting babies into the parental bed or pulling a bassinet alongside it), and "baby wearing" in which infants are literally attached to their mothers via slings.

Attachment parenting dogma also says that "every baby's whimper is a plea for help and that no infant should be left to cry." Sears says, "Parents should respond to all cries immediately since excessive crying can damage the brain and lead to developmental disorders." While statements such as these can and should be scientifically examined for accuracy, my concern is that what this approach seems to be advocating is ignoring the need for generational boundaries and, in my opinion, depriving infants and children of opportunities to develop self-mastery and learn appropriate ways of meeting their own needs. The article in *Time* continues, "the prevalence of this philosophy has shifted mainstream American parenting toward a style that is more about parental devotion and sacrifice than about raising self-sufficient kids." Obviously, I believe the latter to be more appropriate and in the best interest of the children.

Extensive clinical findings in family therapy clearly indicate the need for establishing and maintaining appropriate generational boundaries. Dr. Robinson felt strongly about this and encouraged parents to establish and maintain clear generational boundaries early on in the parenting process.

Let's briefly look at the various needs and roles of the family subsystems.

Spousal subsystem

This subsystem needs to be marked by mutual respect, and a willingness to accommodate to each other's needs. It needs to provide for and support intimacy and a "haven" where the couple can temporarily retreat from the various stressors of life. The key skills needed are communication and negotiation of conflicts and differences resulting from their respective families of origin, work, interests, other relationships, etc. Ideally, the couple can resolve many of these issues before the first child is born. However, they need to continue to do the work of the spousal subsystem after they become parents. The most effective spousal relationships are symmetrical. The need for a clear boundary around this subsystem is obvious.

Parental subsystem

This is the executive subsystem which needs to be in charge of and take a leadership position in establishing boundaries, setting and monitoring rules, etc. As I previously noted, it is crucial to maintain clear generational boundaries on the part of both mother-child and father-child relationships. Also as previously indicated, parents need to be able to identify the developmental needs and readiness of their children's ability to accept responsibility. Obviously, in a two-parent family, there is also a need for communication and negotiation so that parents can work collaboratively. Since previous comments have identified various parental responsibilities, these will not be repeated at this time. Appropriate boundary setting also is needed to protect from excessive well-meaning interventions into the parental system by grandparents, in-laws, friends, etc. Parenting, at best, is fraught with uncertainty. Excessive advice or second guessing can increase this uncertainty.

Sibling subsystem(s)

When there is more than one child in the family, an opportunity to learn a number of crucial attitudes and skills: loyalty, leadership, cooperation, collaboration, conflict resolution, etc. is provided. Boundaries around sibling subsystems are needed to protect against excessive intrusion from peers and other outside influences. Parents can also intrude excessively, especially in the area of conflict resolution. One of the common interactions seen in family therapy is what we refer to as "triangling." This occurs when two siblings are in conflict and a third person, often a parent, is "triangled" into the situation. If this happens regularly, conflicts often go unresolved and individuals do not learn conflict resolution strategies and techniques. Triangling can, and often does, occur within and among the other subsystems as well as the family as a whole. It is particularly harmful to children when they are triangled into parental or spousal conflicts.

In summary, while each family has a unique structure, research and clinical experience in family development and family therapy suggests that there are optimal patterns of structure in terms of responsible parenting and healthy emotional development. What then, would this "ideal" family look like from a structural standpoint? Its' overall boundaries would be clear and permeable, not overly rigid or diffuse thereby allowing for appropriate interaction with outside "systems" and individuals and entry into and out of the system. Similarly, boundaries around the various sub-systems would also be clear and permeable. Remember, a system carries out crucial functions through its subsystems.

Boundary setting begins with the spousal subsystem. Boundaries and relationships need to be examined and adjusted to allow the couple to accommodate to each other's needs and learn how to communicate and negotiate differences. In boundary setting the couple may be strongly influenced by their families of origin, either in terms of unconsciously gravitating toward a marital relationship similar to their parents or actively striving to create a very different kind of relationship.

The spousal subsystem, as previously noted, needs to be marked by mutual respect in order to allow for mutual accommodation. If this can be accomplished successfully, the marital partners would be ready to assume the role of parents. While the parental subsystem consists of the same two individuals, the roles and responsibilities of the two subsystems are different. As noted, parents need to establish and maintain a position of leadership in the family. In many of the families who have come to see me regarding problems with their children, the parents have literally abdicated authority and responsibility and are unable to regain them. It is upsetting to see parents frantically negotiating with, threatening or bribing young children in order to get them to behave. Young children need to be told what to do until they have the ability to make their own decisions. As will be later discussed this does not imply that we directly control our children but rather that we provide necessary leadership and information.

As children grow and move toward emotional maturity, then negotiation becomes appropriate. The very controlling child is responding to an underlying fear of not being in control and not knowing what to do. Dr. Robinson had very strong feelings in this regard. An effective spousal and parental subsystem are also necessary in order to ensure appropriate sibling subsystem boundary setting and maintenance. Previously I noted that children can learn skills of communication, negotiation and problem solving as well as feelings of loyalty and commitment by functioning within sibling subsystems. However, this is unlikely to happen if parents are frequently intrusive in areas of sibling differences. I previously stated my feeling regarding sibling subsystem "violations."

Last, but certainly not least, individual subsystems boundaries also need to be clear and permeable. This allows for the establishing and maintaining of each individual's unique talents, interests, and identity and meeting individual needs. Each of us requires a provision for personal "space" and respect. Dr. Robinson believed that this over intrusion into individual functioning often begins very early in the parenting process with excessive handling of infants and children and being overly responsive to their demands.

In addition to promoting and maintaining a functional structure, parents need to take a leadership role in establishing effective patterns of communication within the family system. Healthy family functioning requires patterns of communication that will enable the family to accomplish individual and systemic goals and maintain family unity even during stressful situations. Communication needs to be clear, logical, and unambiguous. The family system needs to incorporate mechanisms for negative feedback to minimize change and maintain the basic integrity of the family and those for positive feedback to allow for change when appropriate.

There is a good deal of evidence that communication is a skill that can be taught. Since family structure is largely maintained by the ongoing patterns of communication, changing communication can help a family to redefine, strengthen or perhaps loosen boundaries when necessary to do so. When family members acknowledge that they cannot effectively communicate with each other, this can signal either disengagement and unresponsiveness to individual needs or a blurring of boundaries that allows for children to speak to and argue with parents as if they were speaking to peers.

For many generations, communication between parents and children was mostly "one-way." Parents talked to, as in giving "a good talking to" or they talked at their children. Children were not particularly encouraged to give feedback or to engage in ongoing dialogue with their parents. While this worked reasonably well in some ways, as individuals became better educated and sophisticated, the need for some changes in parent-child communication became obvious.

In 1965, Haim Ginott wrote a book entitled *Between Parent and Child*, which, with over 500,000 hardcover copies sold, became the number one bestseller of the decade and the most famous book in America on the relations between parents and their children. Ginott proposed a new code of communication: "The new code of communication with children is based on respect and skill. It requires (a) that messages preserve the child's as well as the parent's self-respect and (b) that statements of understanding *precede* statements of advice or instruction."

In explaining the need for this approach, Ginott continues, "When a child is in the midst of strong emotions, he cannot listen to anyone. He cannot accept advice or consolation or constructive criticism. He wants us to understand what is going on inside himself at that particular moment. Furthermore, he wants to be understood without having to disclose fully what he is experiencing. It is a game in which he reveals only a little of what he feels, needing to have us guess the rest." Ginott also offered a number of specific examples of how and how not to use praise and criticism with children as well as techniques for disciplining and dealing with behavior problems. *Between Parent and Child* in my opinion continues to be a very helpful resource book for any parent.

In my experience, Ginott's suggested technique of communicating with children can be very effective. It is consistent with research cited by Goleman and others which notes the importance of empathy in establishing and maintaining healthy relationships. Can you remember times in your life when you felt you were truly understood by another person? This would be especially powerful if you were upset or troubled. More than likely if you did experience such an encounter that you felt, and perhaps still do, feel a special connection to that person. Children, due to their less than fully developed emotional functioning, respond particularly well to expressions of empathetic understanding.

Perhaps the next most significant development in parent education occurred when Thomas Gordon published *Parent Effectiveness Training* (PET) in 1970. The book and subsequent training by Gordon and his associates led to a large number of PET groups across the United States. I used many of his concepts in the parent education groups that I led in the 1970's and found them to be helpful. Gordon also advocated "The Language of Acceptance," using a skill he called *active listening*. Through active listening, the parent is demonstrating his or her acceptance of the child and consequently the child will be much more likely to communicate his or her feelings and concerns." Active listening is most appropriately used when the child reveals he has a problem. Usually, parents will spot these situations because they will hear the child express feelings.

In terms of communication, Gordon pointed out the destructive nature of "put-down" messages. He proposed more effective ways of confronting children. He distinguished between "You-messages" and "I-messages." An easy way for parents to be shown the difference between ineffective and effective confrontation is to think of sending either "You-messages" or "I-messages." When I have asked parents to examine examples of ineffective messages, they are surprised to discover that almost all begin with the word you or contain that word. These Gordon referred to as "You" oriented messages. He explained, "But when a parent simply tells a child how some behavior is making the parent feel, the message generally turns out to be an 'I-message.'" In PET classes parents would practice sending I- rather than You-messages when confronting or correcting their children. I can tell you from personal experience, I-messages are more effective and do help to preserve the child's and parent's sense of self- respect.

Naturally, our style of communication changes somewhat as children grow older. However, the basic rules of Ginott's code of communication and Gordon's, "language of acceptance" should apply if we truly want to keep the lines of communication open with our children (and our spouses). If these lines have been kept open, conflict resolution will be greatly enhanced, particularly with adolescents. Gordon also offers a number of suggestions for resolving parent-child or parent-adolescent conflicts which are included in *Parent Effectiveness Training*, another work that I believe continues to be a good resource for parents.

Conducting family therapy sessions provides a rare opportunity for live observations of family communication. It becomes very clear who communicates with whom and in what manner. It is also helpful to observe the reactions of other family members who are not directly involved in the communication. As I earlier indicated, often when two individuals are in conflict or disagreement, a third party may get "triangled" into the discussion. The initial disagreement would often go unresolved.

This "triangulation" is one of the most potentially destructive forms of communication. When observed in therapy, triangulation would be pointed out and family members would be encouraged to persist with one-to-one communication and triangling would be blocked. Another particularly unhelpful form of communication is when family members talk about each other rather than to each other. Again, in therapy, they would be directed to talk to each other rather than about each other. Murray Bowen, one of the most influential figures in the family therapy field, tells a story about going home to visit his parents after having been on his own for some time. Perhaps because he was now a rather famous psychiatrist, his parents, in turn, complained about each other to him. Bowen's response to these complaints was simply "why don't you talk to each other regarding these problems?"

Another potentially very harmful kind of parent-child communication is sending conflicting or "mixed" messages. A number of studies have found that the frequent use of these contradictory messages is prevalent in families with children with emotional problems. Since we communicate both verbally and non-verbally, mixed messages occur more frequently than we might think. For example, consider the overly enmeshed parent sending a young child off to school and telling the child not to worry about Mommy or Daddy but indicating by facial expression, tone of voice or body posturing that the child should indeed worry. I have seen this pattern more than once in cases of school refusal (which used to be called school phobia). Since children are not free to live independently, these conflicting messages may occur with redundancy and can significantly impair their emotional development.

Essentially, all behavior is communication at some level. We cannot not behave and therefore we cannot not communicate. As parents we need to be aware of the messages we are continually sending to our children and evaluate the consequences of these messages. As Glasser has suggested we need to ask ourselves, "'If I do this or say this will we be closer or farther apart?' The relationship should always take precedence when communicating."

In summary, I believe parents need to accept responsibility for establishing and maintaining healthy structure and patterns of communication within the family system. As noted above, structure and communication are closely interrelated. However, I believe we need to carefully monitor and adjust both when necessary as the family moves through its various developmental stages.

Individuation/Differentiation

Earlier I stated that, in my opinion, many books about parenting fell short of the mark. While several offer what on the surface appears to be good advice, the ability of parents to consistently use this advice receives little attention. In order to help our kids grow up, we need to grow up ourselves. While this statement may seem obvious or even cliché, many of us are not aware of what growing up involves. Much of growth and physical maturation occurs spontaneously.

However, Bowen points out in order to develop into healthy, emotionally mature adults we need to go through a process of *self-differentiation*. This differentiation occurs on two levels, differentiation between thoughts and feelings and differentiation between ourselves and others. An important developmental task is rising above the powerful emotional forces in the family we grew up in and developing our own identity. In other words, according to Bowen, we need to negotiate our way out of our family while still maintaining emotional contact with them. Some readers may have been able to individuate easily and automatically in their families. If this is what occurred in your case you were very fortunate to have had self-differentiated parents who likely grew up with self-differentiated parents. Unfortunately, this doesn't happen often. There are research studies that suggest this happens in about fifteen percent of families, even in middle to upper middle class, well-educated families.

What does it mean to be self-differentiated or "individuated?"

In simple terms this refers to being able to take care of yourself emotionally as well as physically and financially, to be able to stand on your own two feet, have your own opinions, and make appropriate decisions and choices, even when facing powerful emotional pressures. Since the process of differentiation occurs in concert with negotiating our separateness from our family, we need to eventually be able to see ourselves on equal footing with others in our family of origin.

Bowen believed that the family is "an emotional universal and transgenerational phenomenon". In short, he believed that a family's emotional system includes previous generations as well as extended family. Since the process of differentiation of self includes differentiation from others and the differentiation of feeling processes from intellectual processes, it is not surprising that only a small percentage of individuals achieve what Bowen called a "solid self" which he notes "operates on the basis of clearly defined beliefs, opinions, convictions, and life principles developed through a process of intellectual reasoning and the consideration of alternatives." Since the emotional pressures in a family can be very powerful, as parents we need to recognize this and help our children to develop these intellectual processes. If we leave our family of origin with what Bowen referred to as a "pseudo-self" we remain fused to our family and will be likely to remain over-reactive emotionally throughout our lives. Also, we are likely to choose a mate who is also fused to his or her family and transmit this lack of differentiation to our children.

Achieving a solid self requires courage, opportunity, and support. Parents also need to have the courage to allow and help their children to differentiate physically and emotionally. One of the most important things we can teach our children is how to think. Emerson considered thinking to be the "hardest task in the world." He added, "that's why so few do it." Thinking involves a number of difficult intellectual processes. We need to help our children not to be afraid to think since thinking can be scary at times. Obviously if we have helped our children to become self-disciplined, they are much more likely to persist in learning to think. This also requires self-discipline on our part in helping our children to develop their intellectual processes, we need to carefully listen to them and help them to see both sides of any issue or decision and learn to prioritize. Perhaps most importantly we need to allow them to make decisions when they are able to do so rather than making decisions for them. Remember, we are not raising children we are raising future adults. The goal should be to prepare them for a happy, successful life after they are with us as well as when they are living with us. I frequently reminded parents that what we were doing in child rearing was preparing our children to leave.

One of the measures of how "grown up" we feel is in our ongoing relationships with our parents. Do we feel like we are on the same level or do we find ourselves feeling subservient and immature in their presence. A former colleague of mine who is very successful professionally and has even gained national recognition told me the following. He would visit his family on holidays or special occasions. Each time they would end up going out to dinner at least one night. At the end of the dinner his father, a rather powerful figure, would insist on paying the check. He told me when this happened he felt like "a little kid who couldn't take care of himself." Finally, he decided after one of these dinners he would pay the check regardless of how strongly his father protested. He said he was prepared to "go to blows" if this became necessary. His father relented and he paid the check. I saw him soon after and he told me he couldn't believe how "liberated" he felt. He got the feeling his father finally saw him as an adult. While I am not suggesting that achieving differentiation can be accomplished in one encounter, however, I believe his experience highlights the need we all have to be seen as mature adults, especially by our parents, and the fact that we sometimes need to take risks to accomplish this task. I have coached several clients in identifying and implementing little changes in their relationships with their parents that would have powerful symbolic significance. As I indicated earlier, "change begets change."

Bowen further believes that we tend to choose a mate who is roughly at the same level of differentiation as we are. If the undifferentiation carried over from both partners families of origin is substantial, Bowen believed what he called a multigenerational transmission process would take place where in this immaturity is projected onto their children, in particular the child or children most problematic or most involved in the family's emotional process. That child or children's problems would be passed on to future generations. If you and your mate both identify the need for more differentiation, you can help each other through the "unfinished business." If one or another partner is somewhat farther along in differentiating, they could gently coach their partner in the process. My experience is, however, similar to Bowen's in that spouses tend to be at roughly the same level. We would be quite uncomfortable interacting intimately with someone who is at a very different level.

It is important to realize that things are often not what they seem. The "rugged" individualist or overly opinionated person may, as Shakespeare would suggest, be "protesting too much" in response to underlying insecurities about not having achieved individuation. For Bowen, families function best when both parents are reasonably well differentiated, and the system allows for children to become differentiated as well. As previously noted, he also felt it was important for parents to differentiate from but maintain healthy emotional contact with their families of origin.

The Family Life Cycle

Carter and McGoldrick conceptualize a family life cycle and note key points in the developmental process while individuals and families are transitioning through the various stages. They also identify changes in family status required to proceed developmentally and function appropriately. They refer to "second-order" changes (i.e. changes in the system itself) to allow for appropriate development. Their view is that "family" comprises the entire emotional system of at least three and now frequently four generations: "'family' comprises the entire emotional system of at least three and now frequently four generations. Thus, although we recognize the dominant American pattern of separately domiciled nuclear families. They are, in our views emotional systems, reacting to past, present, and anticipated future relationships within the larger three generations family system." They continue, "But the tremendous life-shaping impact of one generation on those following is hard to over-estimate. For one thing the three or four generations must accommodate to life cycle transitions simultaneously. While one generation is moving toward older age, the next is contending with the empty nest, the third with young adulthood, forming careers and intimate peer adult relationships and having children and the fourth with being inducted into the system." It is my contention that we need to be aware of and accept being a part of this overall multigenerational family and be aware of the challenges of the various stages and the effect on our nuclear families and on us as individuals.

In the family therapy course I initiated and taught to graduate students at the University of Scranton, I required them to do a detailed investigation of their family of origin. Again, viewing family as consisting of at least three generations. Most students were able to obtain information from four or more generations. Amazingly, one student was able to obtain extensive information for eight generations. She grew up in India and her family had lived in the same village for those generations. She and her sister were the first to leave when they came to America. Virtually all students reported this exercise was very helpful. If you do not have a detailed family history, I suggest you consider doing some basic research. Almost all communities have genealogy research centers. *Ancestry.com* is an excellent website.

CASE EXAMPLES

In working with many families, I have observed a number of clear-cut examples of both disengagement and enmeshment. Two rather classic examples come to mind. Hopefully, these examples will illustrate the importance of viewing families systemically rather than assigning blame to various individuals within the family. Before we look at the cases, just a brief comment regarding my approach to family therapy.

One of my firm ground rules in working with families was that everyone living in the family's house had to be present at the first session. After the first session, I would decide which members had to attend for subsequent sessions.

Freud believed that the first treatment session was very important for seeing the patient as they truly were, because defense mechanisms were usually not fully mobilized. I agree and find this is particularly true for families. In the first session my primary goals were to gain each family member's perception of the presenting problem and to "read" the system. Reading the system included observing various alliances, coalitions, communication patterns, feedback mechanisms and boundaries. In my mind everything that happened in the first session became "grist for the mill" in terms of developing strategies for intervention. I always began by asking each family member the same question "How do you see the problem that brought you here today?" Everyone, with the exception of very young children would be expected to respond. Glasser's control theory tells us that our behavior is an attempt to control for our perceptions. This theory will be noted in a subsequent chapter. However, I believe that how family members answered that question gave me insight into how they had been addressing the problem in addition to gaining an understanding of the family's structure and dynamics.

One of the basic principles of family therapy is that the therapist must join the family before being in a position to affect any real change in the system. Obviously, some families are more likely to allow this to happen than others. I had to devise strategies for families allowing me to enter the family system and to temporarily, at least, becoming an integral part of the family. In the two examples, joining with Family A was more problematic than joining Family B for a number of reasons.

To come back to my first question, when working with a two-parent family, I always asked the father first. Fathers generally want to be seen as the head of the family. Also, fathers are usually somewhat less likely to act as family spokespersons than mothers.

Family A – "Boys Will Be Boys"

This family was referred for treatment by a Juvenile Court Judge. Their 17-year-old son, Robert, along with another boy set fire to two large trucks causing thousands of dollars of damage. The judge was seriously considering sending Robert to a Juvenile Detention Center and was awaiting the outcome of treatment and my recommendations before making his decision.

Robert was seen with his father, mother, his 19-year-old sister, Judy and his maternal grandmother. When I asked his father how he saw the problem, he responded, "boys will be boys." His mother's tearful answer to the first question was, "I don't want him to go to prison." Judy and Robert's grandmother gave similar responses. Robert's response was "I don't know. I'm scared." The rest of the first session consisted of information gathering and planning for future sessions. I obtained permission to contact Robert's guidance counselor which was standard practice for me.

As I continued to work with the family, it was important for me not to assign blame for Robert's problem to anyone, especially to his obviously disengaged father. Instead, I looked at each of the family's subsystems' boundaries to determine which might need to be strengthened and which would need to be weakened. Having read the system I concluded that the father/son and marital subsystems were disengaged. It also appeared after two sessions that there was somewhat of a coalition consisting of the three female family members and the sibling subsystem was also disengaged. On Robert's part he remained distant from the rest of the family.

Fortunately, the judge had mandated the family continue in treatment, and I continued to require all family members to be present. For the first two sessions Robert's father was, at best, a reluctant participant as was Robert. The other family members participated well. I was trying to devise ways in which I could join with Robert and his father when I got a lucky break. When the family came in for the third session, the father was wearing an army fatigue jacket. I commented on that and asked about his military service. He responded readily and asked if I had been in the military and I told him I had. The importance of this was this gave the father a sense of recognition and his participation and his relationship with me showed rapid improvement. He spoke of his concern for his son and his desire to help him. I asked him if he could schedule some activity with Robert for the following week. He and Robert agreed to spend some time together in the father's workshop. The father was reported to be very skillful at woodworking. I next scheduled sessions for just Robert and his father, and these went well. His father helped him get a part time job and their relationship clearly strengthened. Full family sessions were intermittingly scheduled but I also scheduled two sessions with Robert and Judy which also went well. Robert was seen for three individual sessions and one session with just his parents. When Robert and the whole family continued to be doing well, I scheduled some sessions for the father and mother.

A number of issues were addressed including the mother's need to strengthen the boundaries between herself and her mother and her over-involvement with her daughter. The couple also addressed some spousal issues.

In short, in a matter of less than three months, the family made significant changes in the overall system and in the various subsystems. Robert's guidance counselor reported his school behavior was excellent and his achievement was improving. I was able to report these positive behaviors to the judge who placed Robert on probation rather than juvenile detention. I scheduled periodic follow up sessions with the family and they continued to do well in a number of areas.

Family B – "Breakfast in Bed"

Family B was self-referred. They were concerned about their son, Kevin, age 14, who was seriously underachieving in school despite doing well on standardized tests. He was also having some social issues and minor disciplinary problems in school. Kevin was seen with his parents and his 17-year-old sister, Susan. When asked how he saw Kevin's problems, his father replied in a rather superior, hostile tone, "his mother treats him like a 5-year-old." I asked for some clarification and he added, "she serves him breakfast in bed." Kevin's mother admitted that was true because, "she wanted to be sure he was well nourished and got to school on time." When asked, Kevin's sister, Susan, strongly agreed with her father's assessment of the problem. Kevin's response to my initial question was, "I just don't like school; I wish I didn't have to go."

An initial reading of the family system provided some apparent imbalances in a number of subsystems. Kevin and his father were clearly disengaged, and the marital subsystem was disengaged as well. Kevin's mother was enmeshed with him, and there also appeared to be an enmeshed father/daughter relationship. The sibling subsystem was also disengaged. Subsequent questions and discussions during the first two sessions confirmed my initial impressions. Fortunately, Kevin's parents were highly motivated to continue in treatment. His father, a very successful executive, was particularly upset about Kevin's poor academic achievement. His mother's motives were more complex, but she was also very anxious to continue.

When I looked at the various subsystems in terms of points of intervention, I chose the sibling subsystem as a beginning strategy. While perhaps less significant in the overall picture, I saw this the least threatening to the family system. I scheduled two sister/brother sessions and was pleasantly surprised with the results. Susan reached out to Kevin and he responded, reluctantly at first, but some very positive interactions took place. She offered to help him with schoolwork, and they planned some other activities. These meetings also led to numerous insights into the family systems. Kevin admitted to being intimidated by his father but wishing they could do some things together. As you might guess, I next scheduled two father/son sessions which also went well. They planned to play golf together and attend a baseball game (I always gave the family "tasks" for the time between sessions). I also intermittingly scheduled some individual sessions for both Mom and Dad. I strongly encouraged Mom to pursue some of her own interests. She had stopped serving breakfast in bed after the second session. I also scheduled some family sessions, primarily as follow-ups to planned activities or changes. It is very important that when the family agrees to follow through with some plans or tasks that I would check on this in the next session. Finally, I offered Kevin's parents the opportunity to follow through in marital therapy and they agreed. Over a period of time, a number of significant issues were discussed and at least partially resolved. They reported Kevin was doing much better in school and the family was engaged in a number of pleasurable activities together. Reports from Kevin's guidance counselor confirmed his progress in school.

I include these examples to hopefully illustrate the viability of focusing upon family structures, boundaries, and interactional patterns rather than individuals within the family in order to effect change. The next chapter provides an opportunity for you to explore in some detail your experiences within your family of origin.

Key Points Chapter 3

Key Point #1

Our behavior is significantly influenced by the context in which it occurs. While this appears rather obvious, it is easy to lose sight of this in day to day interactions.

Key Point #2

Parents are strongly encouraged to view their families as multigenerational systems rather than as groups of individuals who happen to be related to each other. I suggest briefly reviewing the relevant concepts derived from systems theory and family therapy on a regular basis.

Key Point #3

By focusing on transactional patterns in our families rather than on individual characteristics or behaviors we can discover many potential ways of changing those patterns when it is necessary to do so and avoid placing blame on individuals.

Key Point #4

All families have a structure which is revealed when we look at the dynamic interactions of a family. It is important to evaluate the boundaries around and within our families. Criteria for functional boundary setting and maintenance are noted and should be reviewed on a regular basis.

Key Point #5

Systems carry out their necessary functions through their various subsystems. Criteria necessary for functional subsystems are also noted.

Key Point #6

I believe parents have a responsibility to accept a leadership role in assessing the functionality of the family's overall structure and the various subsystems and making changes necessary to maintain healthy family functioning.

Key Point #7

The need for establishing and maintaining appropriate generational boundaries and allowing for individuation and differentiation is crucial to healthy family functioning.

Works Cited

Bowen, M. (1978). *Family Therapy in Clinical Practice*. New York, NY: Jason Aronson.

Carter, B., & McGoldrick, M. (Eds.). (1988). *The changing family life cycle*. New York, NY: Gardner Press.

Davidson, M. (1983). *Uncommon sense: The life & thought of Ludwig Von Bertalanffy*. Los Angeles, CA: J. P. Tarcher, Inc.

Emerson, R.W. (1985). in *Intellect in the Great Thoughts*. New York, NY: Ballentine Books.

Ginott, H. G. (1965). *Between parent & child*. New York, NY: Avon Books.

Minuchin, S. (1974). *Families & family therapy*. Cambridge, MA: Harvard University Press.

Thomas, G. (1970). *Parent effectiveness training*. New York, NY: Random House.

4

Family of Origin Survey

Up to now, I have offered a number of observations and advice regarding parenting for your consideration. I have also indicated my belief that in order to parent effectively, we need to understand the context in which parenting occurs, most notably our nuclear family and fully appreciate how our experience in our families of origin can influence us in our parenting.

At this point, I would like to suggest we become a bit more interactive. I have put together a number of statements regarding your memories of your family of origin, and your past and current levels of involvement with your family as well as some of your own parental attitudes and beliefs. I have included a number of these statements in what I call the Family of Origin Survey (FOS). This survey has not been standardized or subjected to the rigors of determining reliability or validity. It is not a test and there are no right or wrong answers. The purpose is to provide an opportunity to reflect on your experiences in the family you grew up in as well as on some of your current attitudes and beliefs about parenting.

I am asking you to set aside a little time and find some privacy so that you can complete the survey. If you choose, you can share this with your siblings (not your parents).

Please make a copy of the FOS for your parenting partner if you have one. Again, he or she should complete it independently.

After completing the FOS, I suggest you and your partner discuss your respective responses. In doing so it is important not to engage in "one upsmanship" by focusing on whose family was more functional or healthier, etc.

The ideal time to do this would be before your first child is born. However, I believe this exercise can be helpful at any point in the parenting process.

Self-inventories such as this one are subject to potential response biases. The most likely bias in a survey such as this is what is referred to as the social desirability response set. That is, people tend to respond in a socially desirable way rather than what they really believe or feel. Obviously, this exercise will only be helpful if your responses are to the best of your ability, accurate, and honest.

Why is it important to reflect on our experiences within our family of origin? Simply put, as previously noted, in order to help our children grow up to be responsible adults, we need to grow up ourselves (i.e. reach a level of emotional maturity necessary for responsible parenting). By focusing on our memories and perceptions of our family of origin, we may discover some "unfinished business" in the growing up process. Your responses may help you to assess the degree to which you have "differentiated" as a person in your own right. Also, since parenting involves the blending of both maternal and paternal families into a workable whole, it is important to be aware of differences, similarities, and potential conflicts with our parenting partners as we continue in this "blending" process within our nuclear families. Remember, we may be strongly influenced in our behavioral attitudes and behaviors by these experiences in our families of origin. Often this happens unconsciously. By bringing some of these experiences to a conscious level we may be able to better assess their influences on us.

Family of Origin Survey

	Strongly Agree	Agree	Disagree	Strongly Disagree
There was a strong sense of cohesiveness "we-ness" in my family.	○	○	○	○
There was a strong sense of pride in my family.	○	○	○	○
In times of stress, my family could really pull together.	○	○	○	○
I was always aware of my family as a strong source of support.	○	○	○	○
My family was creative and spontaneous in finding solutions to problems	○	○	○	○
I always felt confident that my family would find solutions to any problems we faced.	○	○	○	○
Everyone's opinions counted in my family.	○	○	○	○
Everyone was given credit for any contributions they made to family wellbeing.	○	○	○	○
My family had very rigid beliefs about most issues.	○	○	○	○
My family's rules were very clear.	○	○	○	○
Punishment for rule violations was consistently applied.	○	○	○	○

	Strongly Agree	Agree	Disagree	Strongly Disagree
Punishment for rule violations was harsh.	○	○	○	○
My parents worked together in enforcing the family rules.	○	○	○	○
My parents spent a lot of time with me and did a lot for me.	○	○	○	○
My family encouraged me to interact with others outside of the family.	○	○	○	○
My parents were readily available to me most of the time.	○	○	○	○
Lines of communication between me and my parents were open.	○	○	○	○
I received a lot of positive reinforcement from my parents.	○	○	○	○
In my family all of the children had specific chores.	○	○	○	○
In my family my parents made sure we completed our chores.	○	○	○	○
My family kept close contact with members of previous generations and extended family.	○	○	○	○
Outsiders were welcome within my family	○	○	○	○

	Strongly Agree	Agree	Disagree	Strongly Disagree
My family didn't like changes in routine or behavior.	○	○	○	○
My parents seemed to have a harmonious relationship.	○	○	○	○
My parents were good communicators and negotiators.	○	○	○	○
We had a lot of fun in my family.	○	○	○	○
My family had strict moral and ethical standards.	○	○	○	○
There was a lot of warmth and empathy in my family.	○	○	○	○
If two people disagreed in my family they could usually work it out without someone else getting involved.	○	○	○	○
In my family we were encouraged to discuss our problems.	○	○	○	○
In my family we were not allowed to openly express anger.	○	○	○	○
In my family we were encouraged to keep busy and not waste time.	○	○	○	○
In my family my parents sacrificed their fun for the children.	○	○	○	○

	Strongly Agree	Agree	Disagree	Strongly Disagree
In my family there was a lot of quarreling and disagreement.	○	○	○	○
In my family honesty and integrity were highly valued.	○	○	○	○
In my family material wealth was highly valued.	○	○	○	○
My family has a strong sense of ethnic traditions and pride.	○	○	○	○
My family placed a high value on neatness and cleanliness.	○	○	○	○
My family strongly valued education.	○	○	○	○
My family strongly valued religion.	○	○	○	○
In my family children were allowed to disagree with parents if they felt their own ideas were better.	○	○	○	○
In my family our parents did their best to avoid any disappointment for the children.	○	○	○	○
In my family children realized how much our parents gave up for them.	○	○	○	○
In my family children were unquestionably loyal to our parents.	○	○	○	○

	Strongly Agree	Agree	Disagree	Strongly Disagree
In my family outward signs of affection were not encouraged.	○	○	○	○
In my family my mother made the rules.	○	○	○	○
In my family my father always knew what was best for us.	○	○	○	○
In my family parents kept out of children's activities as much as possible so that they could learn to do things on their own.	○	○	○	○
In my family our parents made it their business to know everything the children were thinking.	○	○	○	○
In my family children were protected from jobs that would be too tiring or hard for them.	○	○	○	○
In my family spanking and other forms of physical punishment were not allowed.	○	○	○	○
In my family everyone was taught to try hard for success.	○	○	○	○
In my family children were protected from difficult situations.	○	○	○	○

	Strongly Agree	Agree	Disagree	Strongly Disagree
In my family, my parents were usually in agreement about how to deal with the children.	○	○	○	○
My parents appeared to really enjoy each other's company.	○	○	○	○
My parents always treated each other with respect.	○	○	○	○
My parents worked well together as a team.	○	○	○	○
My parents openly displayed affection for each other.	○	○	○	○
My parents rarely argued.	○	○	○	○
Members of my family had a difficult time adapting to change.	○	○	○	○
I believe sometimes it's necessary to sacrifice marital harmony in order to be a good parent	○	○	○	○
I had very good relations with all of my siblings	○	○	○	○
There was a lack of privacy in my family	○	○	○	○
My parents could remain calm in the face of problems and get them resolved	○	○	○	○
I always felt I could go to my parents with any problem	○	○	○	○

	Strongly Agree	Agree	Disagree	Strongly Disagree
My parents always seemed to be able to maintain emotional control even in difficult situations	○	○	○	○
I got a lot of approval and encouragement from my parents	○	○	○	○
There were a lot of "secrets" in my family	○	○	○	○
I was strongly encouraged to act independently by my parents	○	○	○	○
I always felt my opinions and ideas were seen as important by my parents	○	○	○	○
When my parents and I disagreed we could usually find a negotiated solution	○	○	○	○
I feel as if I have a good awareness of my feelings	○	○	○	○
I can usually manage my emotions well	○	○	○	○
I believe I am usually able to understand and respond to others' feelings	○	○	○	○
I usually don't have difficulty motivating myself	○	○	○	○
I believe I am skillful in handling relationships	○	○	○	○
I have fully accepted my parents' philosophy and methods of child rearing into my own parenting	○	○	○	○

	Strongly Agree	Agree	Disagree	Strongly Disagree
I often find myself saying or doing to my children exactly what my parents said or did to me	○	○	○	○
I try hard to live up to my parents' expectations of me as a parent	○	○	○	○
I worry that my parents might not approve of some of my parenting ideas or methods	○	○	○	○
I resent my parents "butting in" and telling me how to raise my children	○	○	○	○
I have pretty much cut off any real emotional contact with my family of origin	○	○	○	○
I feel as if I have a lot of "unfinished business" with my family of origin	○	○	○	○
I always consult my parents about any important decision.	○	○	○	○
I sometimes feel as if my parents see me more as a child than an adult.	○	○	○	○
I find my opinions and beliefs about most things are very similar to those of my family of origin.	○	○	○	○
The family I grew up in was very child centered.	○	○	○	○

	Strongly Agree	Agree	Disagree	Strongly Disagree
In the family I grew up in, children were clearly seen as secondary to the adults	○	○	○	○
My family was very involved in all of my sports or other activities	○	○	○	○
I find the relationship between myself and my spouse is very similar to that of my parents	○	○	○	○
I believe it is important to maintain good emotional contact with one's family of origin	○	○	○	○
I find that as a parent I often become so upset that I just can't think straight	○	○	○	○

Please consider the following open-ended questions as the final part of the FOS:

What member of my family of origin am I most like?

What member of my family of origin am I least like?

Overall, what was the most rewarding thing about growing up in my family?

Overall, what was the most difficult thing about growing up in my family?

```
┌─────────────────────────────────────────────────┐
│                                                 │
│                                                 │
│                                                 │
│                                                 │
└─────────────────────────────────────────────────┘
```

Thank you for completing the FOS! You may want to reward yourself with dark chocolate, a hot bath, or perhaps, a glass of wine.

The survey was designed to give you some additional insight into the structure, dynamics and organization of your family along with some specific patterns of interacting and communicating.

I earlier suggested you compare your results with your partner. As I said, similarities and differences can be discussed and where needed, negotiated. I have observed in most families there is an ongoing (often unconscious) struggle revolving around will our nuclear family be more like yours or mine?

You can also examine structure, communication patterns and dynamics in terms of the ideas presented in the preceding chapter.

One additional observation, if your opinions and child rearing attitudes are very similar to those of the family you grew up in this could signal a lack of differentiation. Individuals who are undifferentiated tend to be more rigid and emotionally dependent on others. Those who are more differentiated can experience emotions but also maintain objectivity and emotional distance when appropriate to do so. They are less prone to being "emotionally hijacked". In addition, they are more likely to allow their children to attain an appropriate level of differentiation.

In looking at your responses to the FOS, I suggest you consider the following questions:

- What have you learned regarding the significant similarities or differences between you and your parenting partner?
- Have you been able to identify the prevailing structure in your respective families? What about patterns of communication and methods of discipline?
- How would you describe the overall emotional climate in your family of origin?
- Did your family facilitate your individual differentiation or did they make it difficult?
- How would you describe your current relationships with various family members?
- To what extent has your current parenting approach been influenced by your experiences growing up?
- Have you identified "unfinished business"? Can you think of ways you might go about addressing this?
- Has this exercise provided helpful insights for your own parenting in your nuclear family?

James Framo, in his book *Family of Origin Therapy*, offers some instruction he gives to clients who are exploring their family of origin experiences: "I instruct the clients to think about the important events that occurred in the family when they were growing up; what the family was like, what were the mysteries, stories, myths and secrets in their family that they wondered about; what questions are stuck in their heads that they always wanted to know but were afraid to ask; and most important, what past or present issues exist with each member of the family?"

Works Cited

Framo, J. L. (1992). *Family-of-origin therapy: An intergenerational approach.* New York, NY: Routledge.

5

Psychosocial Development

It is in the best interest of every parent or prospective parent to become as knowledgeable as possible regarding all aspects of their child's development. Fortunately, there are many good resources available regarding children's physical and cognitive growth and development. The more knowledge we have, the more competent we can be as parents. Dr. Robinson would point out to parents that they need to be cautious in interpreting indicators of "average" or "normal" development. He noted that the range of normality can be quite broad, particularly in the early stages of development.

When a baby enters the family system, the previous structure must adapt to the needs and demands of the child. Erik H. Erikson, one of the foremost figures in psychoanalysis and one of the acknowledged leaders in the study of human development, explains in *Identity & The Life Cycle* that a baby's presence "exerts a consistent and persistent domination over the outer and inner lives of every member of the household" because of its need for caring and attention. He continues, "Because these members must reorient themselves to accommodate his presence, they must also grow as individuals and as groups." Raising a child, then, in Erikson's opinion requires a change in perspective along within ongoing accommodations to the developmental needs of the child.

What I have found to be lacking in parenting literature is reference to and an appreciation of what the child is experiencing on an emotional or psychodynamic level during the various developmental stages. In order to more fully understand the emotional development of our children and the critical aspects of this developmental process, I believe it is necessary to gain some insight into what children are experiencing on a "less-than-conscious," as well as conscious, level. While it may be difficult for us to believe that infants and very young children experience an awareness of their unconscious motives and desires, psychoanalytic clinical findings and theoretical formulations tell us that is in fact the case. Sigmund Freud, the founding theorist of psychoanalysis, has been criticized by some for his emphasis on psychosexual development. Other psychoanalysts have acknowledged the sexual components of child development but have placed greater emphasis on the social development of the child.

One of the leading figures in the latter group was Erik H. Erikson. He presents in his work *Identity & The Life Cycle* a thorough and insightful analysis of the relationship between the unconscious experiences of children and their social/emotional development.

Erikson believed that one of the most important responsibilities of parenting was to promote the development of what he referred to as "a healthy personality." In discussing this trait, he selected a definition of the healthy personality first offered by Marie Johoda at the 1950 Symposium of the Healthy Personality. She asserted, "A healthy personality actively manages his environment, shows a certain unit of personality, and is able to perceive the world and himself correctly." Using this definition as a point of reference, Erikson presented a discussion of the psychosocial stages of child development and how a child's experiences and perceptions contribute to the development of this healthy personality. A full discussion of all these experiences and perceptions is beyond the scope of this book. I will present here a brief overview of Erikson's theory.

Erikson described a series of psychosocial developmental stages, each including what he referred to as a "crisis" that must be satisfactorily resolved before the child can move on to the next stage in a healthy fashion. There is a predetermined sequence in which these stages occur. In my opinion, it is critically important for parents to be aware of their child's stage of development and respond appropriately to the various needs of that stage. As Erikson asserted, "the healthy child, given a reasonable amount of guidance, can be trusted to obey the inner laws of development, laws which create a succession of potential for interaction with those who tend him." Since much of what the child is experiencing occurs at a below-conscious level, parents need to become attuned to the child's innermost expressions, manifestations, and characteristics of each stage.

Basic Trust vs. Mistrust

Erikson's first stage of development is Basic Trust vs. Mistrust, which occurs within the first year of life. Within this context, *basic trust* implies reliance on others and oneself largely beyond conscious awareness. Erikson pointed out that the amount of trust derived from the experience of the first year depends more on the quality of the relationship with the mother or other providers than on the quantity of what is provided. To successfully resolve the developmental crisis of this stage, the children must learn to trust those caring for them and, in turn, acquire trust in themselves. Consequently, provider(s) need to ensure a stable, reliable, and empathetic environment while the infant gradually learns how to deal with both internal and external demands of this earliest stage of growth.

Erikson believed strongly in the child's capacity to grow in a healthy direction without needing excessive external direction.

As noted, given a reasonable amount of guidance, the child can be trusted to obey intrinsic laws which Erikson referred to as the "Epigenetic Principle." Therefore, to foster trust in self, the infant requires a sufficient amount of time alone to learn to become comfortable and safe in his or her environment. This involves coping with inner urges, soothing oneself, and being in a relaxed state—what Erikson described as "prone relaxation." He considered prone relaxation the first developmental "way station." Having achieved that, the child can move toward subsequent way stations like sitting up and standing.

Dr. Robinson believed the first year of life to be crucial in fostering a healthy development. He began working with parents "right out of the nursery." Among his primary assertions was the concern that infants and children are "handled" too much, preventing the development of internalized trust Erikson advocates. Reduced handling can be a difficult learning curve, but it is absolutely crucial for the healthy development of early trust in oneself.

However, it is equally important that the balance between independence and reliance be implemented gradually; both Erikson and Dr. Robinson also cautioned against the danger of abruptly weaning the child from the breast/ bottle and consequently the warm, reassuring presence that accompanies it. Weaning should be a gradual process, consistently executed. If done correctly, a "mutual regulation" between the infant and mother is achieved. If there is a drastic loss of maternal affection without proper substitution, it may lead to "feelings of depression which may become chronic or in some circumstances acute and very serious." Dr. Robinson's recommendations to establish healthy eating and sleeping behaviors early in the development process are discussed in Chapter 6.

Autonomy vs. Shame and Doubt

This stage of development takes place during the second and third years of life. As opposed to the Basic Trust vs. Basic Mistrust stage, where the infant was necessarily almost totally dependent on the caretaker, the child becomes increasingly aware of his capacity to make choices. Specifically, to choose between conflicting impulses of retention and elimination, or as Erikson describes, holding on and letting go. More literally, he is referring to the expulsion of the feces.

The primary developmental (and parental) challenge of this stage revolves around what is commonly referred to as "toilet training." During this process, if the child has a firmly developed sense of early trust, he/she is now experiencing an emerging sense of autonomy. It is somewhat ironic that the more effective the caretaker has been in helping the child to establish a strong sense of basic trust, the more likely the child may be to want to express their autonomy. This whole stage, then becomes a battle for autonomy—a very healthy, if somewhat challenging, ambition.

The approach toward toilet training is therefore highly influential on the child's progression towards autonomy. Parents whose approach to toilet training places a heavy emphasis on authoritarian control are likely to be threatened by the child's struggles for autonomy and may try to "break" the child's will. This can lend to a very contentious and prolonged struggle. The child can alternate between active aggression (going when not supposed to) and passive aggression (refusing to go). Often when this is the case, the child will demonstrate signs of regression to the previous stage of development where his preoccupation was on oral satisfaction and fulfillment. He may also become overly "whiny" and demanding in addition to being combative.

One of the detrimental techniques used by some parents caught up in a struggle with their children is shaming. Erikson noted that far too little attention had been given to the concept of shame in psychology. I strongly agree, having seen numerous examples in my clinical experience of clients who struggled with pervasive feelings of shame. There is emerging research indicating that unresolved feelings of shame can be a factor in addictive behaviors. Erikson vividly describes shame and its affects: "Shame supposes that one is completely exposed and conscious of being looked at in a word, self-conscious." Observed shame-based punishments include name calling, forcing the child to wear dirty diapers, and embarrassing the child in front of others.

While over controlling approaches can be potentially harmful to the child's emerging sense of self, a totally laizze-faire or overly permissive approach can also have adverse effects. The child is at risk of feeling unsupported and perhaps unloved. It is crucial at this stage that the child achieve a sense of self-control without having to lose self-esteem to obtain it. If this is obtained, Erikson notes the child will experience a "lasting sense of autonomy and pride."

Erikson believed the consequences of severe conflicts at this stage can have long lasting, negative effects on personality development, suggesting this stage "can be decisive for the ratio between love and hate, for that between cooperation and willingness, and for that between freedom of self-expression and its suppression." Consequently, Erikson cautions against toilet training being too rigid or too early as this prevents the child from learning to gain gradual control over their bowels and other functions. Erikson's advice to parents can be summarized thusly: "be firm and tolerant with the child at this stage and he will be firm and tolerant with himself. He will find pride in being an autonomous person, he will grant autonomy to others; and now and then he will even let himself get away with something." Dr. Robinson's recommendations regarding toilet training are noted in Chapter 6.

Initiative vs Guilt

Erikson tells us the child of four or five is now faced with the next developmental crisis: "Being firmly convinced that he is a person, the child must find out what kind of a person he is going to be." The child looks for examples of what they may want to become and naturally finds their parents as convenient but rather lofty and unattainable role models; they imagine themselves on unequal footing. Thus begins the very crucial process of identifying with the parents and striving to be like them. This is a great moment of opportunity for parents to begin to develop a life-long, mutually satisfying companionship with their children.

Consequently, parents at this time need to be very aware of their own moral and ethical behaviors since they are serving as the role models (previously, I noted the importance of modeling self-discipline and the various traits identified with emotional intelligence). It is during this stage that the child's conscience becomes firmly established. Erikson saw conscience as the "cornerstone of morality." The development of the conscience is necessary for the children to feel able to depend on themselves and at the same time feel dependable to others. For this reason, the child is ready and able to learn quickly and avidly. They can be guided by the parent into a "more realistic identification based on the spirit of equality experienced in doing things together." This companionship can be a lasting treasure for the parent and child.

The danger for parents at this stage is failing to recognize that the child who is so ready to over-restrict themselves needs time and patience to gradually develop a sense of responsibility. Since the child is striving for some sense of equality with the parents, it is important for parents to be aware of how they can, at times, be unknowingly intimidating and overbearing. Parents must avoid overly restrictive or punitive behaviors. I have often cautioned parents and teachers to be aware of the significance of the size difference between them and their children. I would ask them how they would feel if someone two (or three) times their size was shouting at them threatening them, or just looking disdainfully at them?

Erikson stressed the need for parents to see their children as "equal in worth although different in kind or function or age." If parents can do this, the child will emerge from this stage with a sense of competence and, as Erikson called it, enterprise. Naturally, the child is experiencing an ever-expanding ability to move about freely along with significant growth in language skills. These developments allow them to expand their imagination and sense of enterprise, which can be somewhat scary. Despite these somewhat frightening thoughts and accompanying feelings, the child needs to continue to persist in their quest for realistic ambitions and independence. Listening to the child's fantasies and dreams with an understanding ear can contribute significantly to the sense of enterprise the child is striving for.

Further, Initiative vs. Guilt is also the stage of sexual awareness and curiosity. If parents respond to this emerging sexuality by being overly prohibitive or concerned, long-standing conflicts and difficulties may occur. If, instead, they can see it as a normal part of the developmental process, then the child will as well.

Much has been written in psychoanalysis about the subconscious "Oedipus Complex," wherein children experience sexual feelings toward the parent of the opposite sex and see the other parent as a "rival." The child soon comes to see that they are no match for their rival and reluctantly represses the sexual desires. This represents the child's first real experience of loss – giving up on their quest for something they want but cannot have. Parents may see their child expressing emotional responses associated with loss and need to be supportive and yet help the child to come to terms with the fact that they cannot have this fantasized relationship with their parent. Erikson felt this was crucial to the child's emotional growth and development. This difficult time for the child does, however, present an excellent opportunity for role modeling with the parent of the same sex, deep companionship, and learning appropriate social behaviors. Again, these sexual feelings are understandably repressed and, if parents do not overreact, usually resolved without further issue. The most important consideration for parents is that both boys and girls may be experiencing deep feelings of guilt because of these unconscious, repressed urges.

Industry vs Inferiority

This stage of psychological development lasts significantly longer than the previous stages, from approximately age five to the onset of puberty. Freud noted that in terms of psychosexual development, he considered this to be a "latency" stage, meaning sexual and violent drives are normally dormant at this time having been repressed during the Initiative vs Guilt stage. Children typically are more relaxed and easier to relate to during this stage.

As the child develops, they realize that a real sense of self-worth and competence cannot fully be achieved by parental praise and recognition. They come to the realization that a real sense of wellbeing comes from a sense of being able to accomplish various tasks (i.e. a sense of mastery). Dr. Robinson stressed the need for children to have chores as soon as they were able to complete the assigned tasks. He also recommended expanding the chores as the child grew. This can significantly help the child develop the sense of mastery which Erikson advocates.

In the past, many children learned by observing and working with their parents in rural settings. Since we are no longer an agrarian society, many of us do not have the learning experience that comes with living on a farm. For the vast majority of children, this is a time when they must leave the comfortable supportive environment of their homes and go to school, which Erikson noted seems to be a world unto itself with rules, regulations, expectations, and challenges where the child may experience both achievement and disappointment.

The American elementary education system has vacillated between strict teacher-centered approaches and more liberal, "progressive" models of education. In the teacher-centered approach, emphasis is placed on hard work and strict discipline while the student-centered form allows for more freedom of choice, self-discovery, and personal preference. Both methods work for most children, if not taken to extremes. For example, the more liberal or "playful" approach could lead to failure to learn necessary information or a complacency and boredom from always doing what they "want" to do. The hard work approach may foster a highly dependent approach to learning and an unnecessary and costly self-restraint dampening the child's "natural desire to learn and to work." Ultimately, Erikson believed "children of this age like to be mildly but firmly coerced into the adventure of finding out that one can learn to accomplish things which one would never had thought of by oneself."

Erikson believed strongly in the importance of children having skillful and dedicated teachers, particularly during their earliest school years since they are able to identify individual strengths and weakness of students and provide support, encouragement, and, where necessary, remediation. He also felt it was very important for teachers to be able to identify students with psychiatric problems and help them to receive the appropriate treatment. Erikson noted, as have I, how many successful individuals often speak of at least one teacher who inspired them or identified their hidden talent. Erikson strongly encouraged parents to do everything possible to ensure that their children have good teachers.

I have consulted with school professionals on a number of occasions to help them resolve difficulties that may arise in the "interface" of the family and school systems. To ease and improve the transition, I strongly encouraged parents to get to know as much as possible about their children's school and teachers. To further cultivate this area during my professional career, my colleagues and I conducted a comprehensive study aimed at the prevention of academic and behavioral problems funded by a grant from The National Institute of Mental Health. To increase the role of parental involvement in student performance, we attended Kindergarten registrations in an urban school system and invited parents of registrants to participate in discussion groups aimed at encouraging them to become involved in their children's school experience. Follow up studies showed that the children of those parents who participated consistently did well in school. These parents also remained connected with the school and reported a high level of satisfaction with their children's educational progress.

With the occurrence of school attendance, there is increasing opportunity for interaction with peers—a necessary step in development. Erikson asserts it is important for the child to develop an unbiased and cooperative attitude toward fellow "workers" when working towards a sense of industry. This will be greatly facilitated if the child experiences a comparable attitude in his/ her interactions with parents and siblings.

As Erikson's terminology for this stage implies, the danger of this stage can be a sense of inadequacy or inferiority, which may continue throughout the subsequent developmental stages. The child may be unable to adapt to the school climate. For example, if the boundaries and culture of the family of origin are overly rigid or overly diffuse, the child may not have developed the flexibility needed to adapt to the various rules, regulations, and many social challenges he may encounter. Conversely, the lack of rules and structures at home may make adjusting to the educational system very difficult. For this reason, as noted in Chapter 3, I believe in the importance of maintaining a functional family system to prepare the child for adjusting to the demands of school and community. A child's education should not be limited to the school. Parents need to be teachers as well. Scott Peck suggests that two of the most important things parents can teach their children are how to think and how to listen. By listening, Peck does not exclusively mean passively obeying but also a more active process that, like thinking, would require self-discipline and effort.

Identity vs. Role Confusion

Commonly referred to as pubescence or adolescence, this is a stage of rapid changes. Erickson noted at this stage that, "Childhood proper comes to an end. Youth begins." With rapid physical growth and the emergence of genital maturity, puberty presents numerous challenges. Repressed sexual urges return from the Initiative vs. Guilt stage. The adolescent must find a way to deal with these urges while confronting the social challenges associated with this age. The identity, curated through an accumulation of experiences throughout childhood, solidifies during adolescence.

Much has been written about the importance of self-esteem in identity maturation. Erickson used the term "ego identity" to represent the sense of self-esteem that results from successful passage through the earlier developmental stages. However, Erickson points out, correctly in my opinion, that real self-esteem is the result of wholehearted and consistent recognition of real accomplishment (i.e. achievement that has meaning in the adolescent's own culture). He further notes that adolescents are not fooled by empty praise or condescending encouragement.

As would be expected, there is a very strong, in some instances desperate, need for belonging at this stage. This is expressed in cliques and gangs; the importance of choosing the right companions goes without saying. Adolescents can become remarkably clannish, intolerant, and cruel in the exclusion of others who are different or who do not meet the same criteria for acceptance. Some adolescents may see themselves as failures because they do not fit in and join with others who feel similarly and create what Glasser referred to as a "failure identity." He concluded that, simply put, the adolescent feels he can't be a "nobody" (no sense of identity) and therefore chooses a failure identity over no identity at all. Once seen as a failure by parents or others in authority, the adolescent "perversely obliges by becoming just that." This can and often does lead to disastrous outcomes. Erickson likewise notes, "Youth after youth, bewildered by some assumed role forced on him by the inexorable standardization of American adolescence, runs away in one form or another, leaving school and jobs, staying out all night, or withdrawing into bizarre and inaccessible moods." The current availability of drugs, internet, social media, and additional potentially negative influences significantly heightens the means and accompanying danger for those who choose to drop out or run away, figuratively or literally.

Erickson further tells us it is increasingly important to understand that adolescents choose to stereotype themselves, their ideals, and their enemies as a way of reducing the discomfort associated with the many challenges of this stage. Parents need to try to understand the intolerances of adolescent children and to respond with guidance rather than verbal judgements or prohibitions. He notes it is difficult for children to be tolerant if they do not know who they are or who they will become.

In terms of the adolescent's search for an identity, Erickson believed that the inability to settle on an occupational identity was particularly disturbing to adolescents. This may cause them to overidentify (temporarily at first) with heroes or glamorized (but very difficult to obtain) vocational choices. The area of vocational guidance is, in my opinion, seriously undervalued in our culture and educational systems. There have been moments of national awareness of the need for better vocational counseling. In 1958 when Russia successfully launched Sputnik, there was a strong cry to catch up with the Soviets. Funding was provided for identifying and better educating future scientists and mathematicians through the National Defense Education Act. To accomplish this, many training programs for science and math teachers were initiated. Funding was further provided for training and hiring additional guidance counselors to help students chose the right occupation. Sadly, the support for more and better counseling has faded. The typical counselor is responsible for far too many students and focuses on college counseling when not faced with pressing educational or emotional concerns. Therefore, I would encourage parents to be strong advocates for increased vocational counseling in their schools. In addition, discussing occupational/vocational choices with adolescents at home and providing opportunities for career exploration are strongly encouraged.

Conclusion

Freud, in his only visit to the United States to lecture at Clark University in Massachusetts, was asked what was necessary for people to attain mental well-being. His response was simply "Lieben and arbitten" (*to love* and *to work*). Erickson expands on this: "For when Freud said 'love' he meant the expansiveness of generosity as well as genital love. When he said 'love and work' he meant a general work productiveness which would not preoccupy the individual to the extent that his right or capacity to be a sexual and a loving being would be lost."

Such is the challenge of the Identity vs. Role Confusion stage—to emerge with the ability to love and to work well in order to grow into the first stage of adulthood (Intimacy vs. Isolation). Discussion of these various stages of adulthood is not intended to be a part of this book. However, it should be noted that this first stage of adulthood focuses on the challenge of producing and caring for offspring with a loving partner (i.e. parenthood).

Key Points Chapter #5

Key Point #1

Erikson stressed the importance of trusting the epigenetic principle which emphasizes the child's intrinsic motivation and movement toward healthy growth and development.

Key Point #2

Parents need to trust this principle and be supportive and understanding without being over intrusive or protective.

Key Point #3

Understanding what your child is experiencing on a less than conscious level can greatly enhance your parenting.

Key Point #4

An awareness of the crises at each stage of development is important to assess how well your child is developing psychosocially.

Key Point #5

Attempts to deal with the child's normal striving for autonomy through shaming or other negative behaviors can be very disruptive to the developmental process and harmful to the child.

Key Point #6

Strict prohibitions or overreactions to the child's natural expressions of sexuality should be avoided.

Key Point #7

Children need opportunities to learn how to accomplish tasks in order to develop a strong sense of industry and resultant self-esteem.

Key Point #8

Parents need to be tolerant and understanding of their children at all stages of development, but particularly during adolescence.

Key Point #9

Becoming actively involved in your child's educational process can enhance growth in a number of areas for you and your child.

Key Point #10

Understanding what the child is experiencing on a less than conscious level can greatly enhance our ability to serve as appropriate role models and to establish deep and lasting companionships with our children.

Works Cited

Erikson, E. H. (1994) *Identity & the Life Cycle*, New York- London: W.W. Norton & Company.

6

The Robinson Way

I believe this chapter has to begin with a disclaimer of sorts. While I fully agree with all of Dr. Robinson's advice regarding child rearing, some of the information in this chapter may fall under the realm of medical rather than psychological advice. I am not a physician and am not qualified to give medical advice. I am merely sharing some of Dr. Robinson's recommendations with you. Dr. Joseph Robinson was a board-certified pediatrician. He completed his undergraduate education at the University of Michigan. He earned his medical degree at St. Louis University and completed his pediatric residency at Brooklyn Jewish Hospital. He received numerous awards and commendations during his long career as a pediatrician. Dr. Robinson died in 2008 at the age of ninety.

Clinical Research

Dr. Robinson spoke frequently about his feeling that a pediatric residency really doesn't prepare doctors for dealing with the kinds of issues and questions that parents would bring to a pediatrician's office. In hospital training, residents dealt primarily with medical issues and they learned how to evaluate and treat medical problems.

When Dr. Robinson completed his training, he began his practice with no real sense of how to help parents raise their children. He consulted a number of pediatric textbooks and other sources. He felt that the authors were essentially copying and recopying someone else's work and there was not much originality. He was uncomfortable with the fact that he could not be more helpful to parents. He believed that there had to be more to the "well baby care business." He felt a sense of guilt about not knowing what to tell parents. In his mind he was not giving them their "money's worth." He noted most often the child, thankfully, is perfectly healthy (nurses can give shots, weigh them, etc.). Everything is pretty much standardized. Compounding this is the fact that infants and children can't be placed in a laboratory and divided into control and experimental groups comparing various ways of raising or communicating with them. He concluded that if there was really worthwhile information to be learned and passed along to parents, it had to be learned clinically.

Readers who in the past or are currently in the early stages of childrearing can readily remember your child's visit to a pediatrician. The typical scenario is a large number (perhaps twenty or more) parents and children will be in a waiting room anxiously awaiting their turn to see the doctor or nurse. This type of practice has become the prototype for "well baby" care at the pediatrician's office.

Dr. Robinson's practice differed significantly from that described above. He knew that clinical research, as he called it, would take a great deal of time. "*One patient at a time*" was the rule that he practiced religiously throughout his five plus decades as a pediatrician. Obviously there were significant economic limitations to practicing this way. However, he believed that the benefits both to himself and his patients far outweighed any lost revenue. Only by practicing this way could he learn what was truly happening with the parents and children he served. He created a dialogue with parents that enabled him to ask about daily parent-child interactions and understand their consequences. This clinical research, asking and listening carefully in a non- threatening way, provided the primary source of information from which he could truly provide parent education. He would simply ask what was really going on. If parents felt he was not being accusatory or judgmental they would begin to admit if there was something happening that they were not sure of and that they may have needed help with. He felt that if he asked the questions in the right way, important information would come out. Questions regarding how their child was sleeping and eating were particularly important. He believed these were crucial in helping children to learn self-discipline. Mishandling infants and very young children in those areas can have lasting adverse consequences.

Parents frequently asked him what was "normal:" *How long does a normal baby sleep? How much should it eat? How long should it stay awake?* There are some obvious yardsticks regarding at what age babies should crawl or stand or walk but those are relatively easy things to measure. But if you try to compare an infant that is six pounds at birth with one who is ten pounds at birth, how can you possibly say that they should eat the same amount or eat just as often. Dr. Robinson helped parents to think in terms of a range of normality rather than normal being a specific point. This was necessary for giving parents directions without being too rigid. He helped parents to understand that children have individual differences and they, at time, need to be understood and related to differently. He emphasized the fact that if problems or bad habits were ignored, they could easily become entrenched and be very difficult to reverse. Dr. Robinson estimated it took more than ten years of listening to and advising parents, with many mistakes and false starts in between, before he could really be confident in providing the kind of *parent education* he felt would be truly helpful.

I believe it is important to note here that Dr. Robinson did not begin his clinical research with any a priori or theoretical assumptions. He developed his beliefs experientially by carefully processing information obtained from parents regarding their interactions with their children and the results of these interactions. While he himself was highly self-disciplined he did not try to impose his own personal beliefs on parents. The fact that he was able to help parents establish parental practices that helped their children establish self-discipline simply emerged from his research. When I think of self-disciplined children, I am reminded of the comments of educational professionals at the conference mentioned in the introduction to this book, they could readily identify "Robinson Kids" when they entered kindergarten. The kids in their words were "totally ready to begin school." Not only were they well-disciplined but, they were seen as happy and well-adapted socially and academically. They apparently would have met many of Goleman's criteria for emotional intelligence. When we consider that a large number of research studies have demonstrated that the first few years of life are crucial in establishing appropriate patterns of social, emotional, and intellectual growth, the fact that the "Robinson Kids" stood out is not surprising. If these patterns are not established very early, some children may be able to still learn to be self-disciplined and responsible, but it will be much more problematic, and the chances of this happening lessen with each passing year.

Dr. Robinson strongly believed that *parents need to be teachers* and that this teaching *begins soon after mother and child come home from the hospital*. Many parents find it hard to believe how early they can begin teaching but by establishing good feeding and sleeping patterns they are helping their children form good habits that will, in most cases, last throughout their lives. They are also eliminating the need for excessive handling and allowing their children to learn many things for themselves. In previous chapters the importance of parents having reached a level of emotional maturity necessary for knowing when children need to be attended to and when they need to be left alone was noted.

One of Dr. Robinson's pet peeves was the fact that many

children are handled far too much. Helping parents *resist the urge toward excessive handling was one of his biggest challenges in working with parents.* When parents would "buy into" his advice in this regard they discovered that children do quite well without a lot of handling. They also would see that over-handling their children was often more in response to their needs rather than those of the child. Dr. Robinson referred to this as *judicious neglect* and this concept became a cornerstone of his work with parents. Remember Glasser's definition of responsibility as the ability to fulfill one's needs, and to do so in a way that does not deprive others of the ability to fulfill their needs. Children need to have the opportunity to learn how to fulfill their needs as much as possible. This will give them a growing feeling of mastery and self-worth and eventually a sense that they are worthwhile to others. Structural family therapy proponents point out the importance of maintaining appropriate generational boundaries. Parents who consistently violate these boundaries deprive children of the opportunity to learn how to investigate their surroundings. If left alone they will start seeing colors, forms, and lights; they can learn how to soothe themselves and if they are not conditioned to being picked up, they'll enjoy looking around and, more often than not, will be perfectly content until they get tired and go to sleep. They will learn to accept and enjoy their crib, even when they are not sleeping.

The first thing that parents can *teach a child is good eating habits.* This is basic and very important because eating habits established in infancy are likely to last throughout life. Dr. Robinson noted parents he worked with made many mistakes in this area. There is no universally accepted way to start feeding a baby. Some pediatricians recommend not starting food for a year. What is most important is *how the parent handles those early days of food feeding.* The results of very poor feeding habits can range from anorexia or bulimia to morbid obesity. For approximately twenty years, in addition to my teaching and clinical work, I served as a psychological consultant for disability determination, assessing literally thousands of individuals with psychiatric problems. A significant percentage of these individuals, in addition to psychological symptoms, had poor dietary habits, which led to obesity, poor nourishment and a number of related medical problems. All of my colleagues have had similar findings in their assessments. Research indicates individuals with serious eating disorders report eating being tied in with parents' happiness and parents' approval or disapproval of them. Obviously, not all babies who are mishandled in feeding develop serious psychiatric disorders. However, many bad habits can be and are developed, often in combination with physical and emotional difficulties.

Some of the most common feeding mistakes Dr. Robinson found included coaxing or "bribing" infants to eat. At times, parents would literally try to force feed due to anxiety about the baby's nutritional well-being. Another frequent mistake was giving infants food with a high sugar content or mixing high sugar foods with cereals or vegetables. Dr. Robinson noted that once they start eating sugar, they may not want to eat meat or vegetables for years. He would suggest one simple gimmick to parents, telling them that they had to be able to stand a little bit of noise. He recommended starting with foods that are not too outstanding in taste. He cautioned against bribery, coaxing or flavoring the food, this would destroy the whole purpose of the exercise. What you are teaching the baby is that when I'm hungry, I'll be glad I'm being fed. Parents have the perfect weapon – *hunger*! When babies are hungry enough, they'll eat anything. The beauty of it is, it lasts about an hour. Parents need to find a way of being patient for approximately one hour and overcome their fear that the child is going to starve to death.

It would go something like this. If the mother offers cereal, the baby may push out its tongue or gag on it. Gagging is not choking so there is no need to panic. At the very first sign of negativism by the baby, stop! Parents should go for a walk, sing to the baby, but wait approximately a half hour and then offer the food again. If it's refused, stall for another half hour. Ninety-nine percent of babies will gobble up anything you give them. Children who are raised this way were very unlikely to become obese according to Dr. Robinson's research. He noted they may get a little pudgy, but they work it off as they grow older. Dr. Robinson found that breast feeding was better than bottle feeding. Normally babies who have no medical problems, if they are fed as much as they want or can hold, are capable of going a minimum of three hours to, believe it or not, up to twelve hours before needing to eat again.

One of the difficulties parents face is determining when the baby is truly hungry and when the baby is responding to colic. Colic is not an old wives' tale. It is defined as a paroxysm of acute abdominal pain. It is considered idiopathic because the cause is not really known. A significant number of full-term infants develop colic. It starts at almost exactly two weeks of age and lasts approximately three months. Colic often becomes one of the most difficult obstacles parents will face in beginning to raise a baby. Dr. Robinson assured parents that infants do not die from it, they're just unhappy. He added, however, the parents may expire from walking all night, taking the baby for rides, etc. With milder colic, infants may have one bad four-hour period every twenty-four hours and it may stop a little short of three months. He found that if the baby has two, three, or four bad periods, the colic will last three months. This is really a critical test of parents' emotional maturity. Many emotionally immature parents might even become physically abusive because of the intensity of the baby's reaction to the colic. When the baby is crying, spitting up, and restless, parents will often try just about anything for a little peace and quiet. The biggest problem from a developmental standpoint is the constant handling or almost constant handling of the baby during the colicky period. By the time the three months are up, a pattern has been established. The baby's crying is legitimate—idiopathic intestinal colic is very painful. However, after the three months when the cramps are gone, the baby has learned when

I cry, I get attention, I get handled, I get something. Often babies are given a bottle or some food. As we've all experienced, if we have a stomachache and if we eat something, we'll feel better temporarily.

Dr. Robinson found that by using medication in the right dose and at the right time the colic could be relieved about eighty percent of the time. The use of the medication can not only provide relief for the baby, but it can cut down significantly on the conditioning that results from "cry and I'll hold you and feed you." Babies who have been so conditioned are constantly sucking on a bottle or pacifier. More importantly those who were overfed during the three months of colic are likely to have problems with weight control their whole lives. The difficulties parents experience in dealing with a baby with colic are magnified when it is a first-born child. It is important to note that while colic starts at two weeks for a full-term baby, with premature babies, amazingly, it starts at the number of weeks the baby is premature plus two weeks. For example, if the baby is four weeks premature, the colic will begin at six weeks.

To return to feeding, Dr. Robinson felt *it really didn't matter which food you start with*. He recommended starting with vegetables or meat. He had parents start many times with meat for premature babies. They tend to be anemic and meat has a wider band of amino acids. He acknowledged it raised a few eyebrows when he suggested starting with meat, but it worked out quite well. If cereal is chosen, for instance, the first feeding might be just a couple of spoonfuls. Just introduce the food and the baby will get the rest of the feeding from the breast or bottle. Each day as the volume of food is increased, the breast or bottle gradually diminishes. This can be a significant "fringe" benefit. You have begun a weaning process slowly and painlessly. This will also help with establishing good sleeping habits.

As previously stated, babies should be fed any time they are hungry, but we need to determine when it is true hunger and when it is colic. Dr. Robinson suggested a yardstick of approximately three hours. If they wake up and appear to be hungry in periods of less than three hours, it will usually be a colicky period. Babies in non-colicky periods may sleep uninterrupted for anywhere from four to eight or more hours. Dr. Robinson said mothers would call and ask if they should let the baby sleep that long. His response was absolutely. If the baby's breathing was normal, his advice was relax and enjoy it.

Once feedings are established it only takes a day or two before, as he put it, "the kid will be eating you out of house and home." Very quickly the breast or bottle become less important. Again, parents would call with concern that since the baby is eating well, they don't want the breast or bottle. This is appropriate, according to Dr. Robinson because solid food would eventually become the diet staple. He was concerned that many babies drink too much milk. He noted that other mammals are much less dependent on milk than many humans. Since we have domesticated cows and refrigeration, milk can become too large a part of the child's diet. Dr. Robinson felt it would not hurt the baby if their diet was solely solid food (I.e. meat and vegetables).

Another issue is that not too infrequently children are milk sensitive and this can lead to a number of serious symptoms. Many years ago, goat milk was used as a substitute for this reason. This has become very expensive but there are synthetic substitutes, soybean, etc. Decreasing milk does not mean the baby will be calcium deficient since all food has some calcium in it and there are a number of sources of extra calcium. Dr. Robinson believed breast or formula feeding should not last more than six months. Remember with colicky babies, establishing good eating habits will be more challenging and will require more self- discipline on the part of the parent. Dr. Robinson believed babies should begin vitamins when feeding is started.

In establishing good sleeping habits, Dr. Robinson's belief was that judicious neglect was especially important. He believed it was necessary to learn how to ignore the child at the right time. His advice was that if you know the baby is not sick and you leave them alone, you're not going to hurt them. Sleeping habits should be established at three months or very close to that time. If the child has good colic control, the training is obviously easier than with a colicky child. He recommended the following routine. Feed the baby at dinner time, give him or her a bath, let some time pass, put him or her in the crib and get out! This takes courage. Some children with a lot of stamina may cry for an hour but it's important to wait the child out. Dr. Robinson would tell parents they needed courage, stamina, and two deaf ears. As long as the baby has the stamina to keep screaming, they aren't exhausted and won't be hurt. One possible obstacle is that some boys get hernias. These are not caused by crying; they are defects that were there but may show up somewhat sooner if they scream for an extended period of time. Dr. Robinson did not believe that this would be a good reason not to train the child into good sleeping habits.

Dr. Robinson felt it *was important to do the sleep training in the evening*. If this is tried after breakfast, for example, children may have boundless stamina. He said some are "Olympic material" and may cry continuously until lunch time. One reason why the evening is better is because once the baby goes to sleep there should eventually be a period of approximately twelve hours of sleep. Some babies can go as long as fourteen hours. Most mothers, he said, would go in a couple of times each night to make sure the baby wasn't kidnapped, that's how quiet they were. Once the sleep pattern is established, you can resume the same routine in the morning and after lunch naps. The vast majority of babies will accept this very graciously, according to Dr. Robinson's research. The morning naps usually last for a year to a year and a half. The after-lunch nap will last almost until four years of age.

The primary purpose of judicial neglect is to begin to establish what Dr. Robinson called *a disciplinary "atmosphere."* Instead of by shouting or screaming and ranting and raving, discipline is established naturally through good feeding and sleeping habits. Not only will this make parenting less stressful and painful for parents, but you are laying the groundwork for children to establish self-discipline. Dr. Robinson's goal for parents was to have both feeding and sleeping habits established by approximately the end of the third month for babies with good colic control. For those whose colic continues for three months, training can begin at three months. Remember colic can be treated with medication.

Some parents expressed concern that with an attitude of judicial neglect, babies wouldn't get enough nurturing or physical contact with them. Dr. Robinson pointed out that in early infancy there would be four feedings a day which would take an hour each and would include some handling, talking to the baby, hugging and kissing, etc. Washing and bathing and diapering also take time and involve handling. He saw this as a reasonable amount of attention for the early stages of infancy. When the baby is placed in the crib, he or she will be content to roll around and explore their environment. Incidentally, the more you leave them alone, the more adventurous they'll be. Everybody thinks babies need to be taught how to crawl or stand. Unless they have some sort of disability, babies will crawl along, stand up, let themselves down, learn to roll from their belly to their back and vice versa.

Dr. Robinson did not recommend giving babies a bottle in the crib for several reasons. There is a danger the baby could vomit and aspirate and develop pneumonia. If they have a bottle in the crib and are sleeping on and off, they are more prone to other less serious infections such as thrush. In addition, going to bed with a bottle Is not consistent with good eating habits because the more they suck on milk all night long, the more adverse effect on their next feeding. Children who do this will often refuse food and want to have a bottle between feeding and this can destroy the established eating pattern. Babies should also sleep on their stomach rather than their backs.

While discipline can be established with early infants through good eating and sleeping patterns, as they grow older children will obviously present with more situations requiring discipline. Kids can become destructive and dangerous to themselves or others. Screaming and, of course, hitting are not recommended as disciplinary techniques. Parents who resort to hitting usually have to increase the intensity as children grow older and are less intimidated. In addition, they are setting aggressive role models and research indicates children who are disciplined this way are more aggressive toward their peers. Shouting also often needs to become progressively louder. When frequently used, shouting cuts off communication between parent and child.

Dr. Robinson preferred what he referred to as *positive discipline*. He suggested when the child is old enough and understands verbal communication, the parent should say, very firmly and quietly: "stop it or I'm going to punish you." This should not be done for every little negative thing the child does but should be reserved for when punishment is really merited. His rule of thumb was if he or she is doing something you don't like today and you're not going to like it tomorrow or anytime, then it's punishable. If after telling the child to stop or they will be punished, the unacceptable behavior occurs again, march them to a corner. Do not choose a soft chair or sofa, tell the child to stand in the corner. This will be very uncomfortable. As Dr. Robinson put it, "it's like sending him to Siberia." Don't expect this to be accepted gracefully. Take a chair and let them know you're not going anywhere, and you'll kill the whole day if you have to. Expect an argument and tears but stick to your guns. The fight usually lasts about three minutes. After the fight, you may get a new approach; "Mom, I'm sorry, I promise I won't do it again, can I go now." Don't be swayed by this. Let them stand there until really uncomfortable. If it isn't unpleasant, it isn't punishment. How long is unpleasant? Dr. Robinson recommended five to ten minutes. This will seem like an eternity for the child.

You can start using this form of discipline at about one and a half to two years of age at that point the child should be able to stand well. If this is done correctly, you will rarely need to use it as the child grows older because you've proven you mean it. At first you may have to gently restrain them. One mother told Dr. Robinson "he bites me." He told her to take her hand away. Parents need to use their own judgment concerning any modifications of this approach, but it is crucial to institute the disciplinary process early. The longer you wait to do this, like eating and sleeping habits, the more difficult it will become. Dr. Robinson was careful to point out that this should be done quietly and calmly without expressing anger or "put downs." Like Glasser, Dr. Robinson strongly believed in not using forms of discipline that would have long term negative effects on the parent-child relationship.

Dr. Robinson believed *potty training should be a natural process* rather than one that is marked by anxiety and excessive parental pushing. He found parents could accomplish this in a casual way by relying upon the fact that babies have natural bowel movements after feeding. This is called a gastrocolic reflex where the stomach stretches and stimulates the anus. He found the earliest potty training could begin is when the child can sit well, usually at least six months of age and preferably closer to nine months old. If the child can sit erectly without waddling all over the place, just place the baby on the potty. If they have a bowel movement fine, don't make a big deal of it; just say good job. If the child reacts negatively, stop and try again at a later time. The key is to not overreact positively or negatively. Children will fight or resist parents who become hyper and push too hard to the point where they may develop chronic constipation.

Freud believed struggles in this developmental period, which he referred to as the anal stage of psychosexual development, can be very intense and can lead to a number of long-standing problems. Erik Erickson modified Freud's theory by giving the ego more autonomy in development, as previously noted, this second stage of psychological development was referred to as "Autonomy vs. Shame and Doubt." Both theories underscored the psychological significance of parent-child interactions revolving around potty training. Shaming children into forced potty training can create a lingering sense of anxiety and self-doubt along with shame. Dr. Robinson counseled parents to not be too bashful about their own personal toileting habits since these are perfectly natural. You can let kids keep you company in the bathroom. Don't invite them in but simply leave the door ajar. If they want to come in and watch you shave or go through other toileting fine! If not, forget about it. Dr. Robinson recommended parents keeping a low profile.

As previously noted, kids are great mimics. Dr. Robinson reported some younger children virtually toilet trained themselves by observing their parents or older siblings. The most important advice to parents regarding potty training was not to over-push. Believe it or not children are also pushing toward a beginning sense of autonomy. If they feel this is threatened, they can become very stubborn. If intense struggles regarding potty training ensue, both parent and child end up losing. Some children will be bed-wetters. These children have congenitally small bladders and are very sound sleepers. Using shaming, bribery, or continually waking the child can create a psychogenic enuresis. He again recommended maintaining a low-profile approach.

Dr. Robinson followed his patients as they reached adolescence and even into adulthood in many cases by keeping in touch with their parents. He found that by having established self-discipline early in life they generally did not develop serious problems later on. Perhaps as Peck would suggest the discipline enabled them to solve whatever problems they encountered. Children whose parents later divorced also appeared to generally deal with this without severe adjustment reactions. One of Dr. Robinson's former patients told me she was amazed at how well her children handled her divorce. Parents reported that when conflicts with their adolescent children occurred, they were generally resolved without a lot of hostility or emotional distress.

Dr. Robinson told me *his goal in working with children was to help them develop emotional maturity*. He stated this was a combination of things, including learning to accept responsibility and learning the "give and take" of life. He felt it was also crucial that parents modeled these behaviors and helped their children to develop a sense of humor. He defined this as being able to laugh at yourself. If parents can model this, children will pick it up. The psychologist Abraham Maslow extensively studied the process of self-actualization. He found that individuals who met the criteria as "self-actualizers" consistently demonstrated a "non-hostile" sense of humor.

Dr. Robinson *stressed the need for children to have chores*. By age four, or perhaps three with precocious kids, they are ready for a daily job (e.g. making a bed, dusting, putting away toys). Parents were instructed to monitor the completion of these chores. Since kids generally want to do things, they should be told this is their contribution to the family. He did not recommend paying them. Parents reported that once kids bought into the idea of chores, they enjoyed them and took pride in their work. Glasser's belief that we have an inherent need to feel we are worthwhile to others would support Dr. Robinson's approach.

Dr. Robinson obviously recognized the importance of education and the need for parents to encourage and support their children as far as their ability and talents will allow. As he followed up on his patients and former patients, he was pleased with their progress. In general, they demonstrated an ability to persist in the face of difficulties and to tolerate setbacks well in all areas of their lives.

I have been able to interview a small number of parents who worked with him and two of his former nurses. I was very impressed with the gratitude and admiration they expressed toward Dr. Robinson. Several told me how much they loved him. One of his nurses noted that what she admired most about him was that he always acted upon what was in the best interest of the child. She told me that he didn't believe in "schmoozing" parents. He at times was very direct and somewhat authoritarian. Knowing Joe, I can picture him being that way, but always with a twinkle in his eye and a sense of humor. He took his responsibility as a parent educator very seriously. Since he had carefully conducted his clinical research, he believed very strongly that what he had learned would be in the best interest of the child. He required a commitment from parents to try their best to follow his advice. In the process of conducting his clinical research, he established ongoing relationships which were unique in the usual realm of doctor-parent relationships and which were highly valued by those to whom I spoke. One of his former patients is a secretary in the department where I work as a consultant. Her children were also Robinson patients. She is certainly a testimony to his parenting methods. Everyone in the agency marvels at her attitude, organizational skills and her work ethic. She has a sister and two daughters who are also excellent examples of "Robinson Kids."

As I attempted to share some of Dr. Robinson's beliefs and teachings in this book, I marveled at the wisdom of it all. Obviously, my referring to the work of Glasser, Peck, Goleman, and Covey, among others, reveals my theoretical biases. I find it truly amazing how consistent Dr. Robinson's beliefs regarding responsibility, discipline, and healthy adaptive behavior were with their beliefs. I am convinced that any parent who would follow his advice would benefit greatly, as would their children. He himself referred to his work with parents as "preventive psychiatry." I could not agree more.

While Dr. Robinson's primary concern was children, he also cared deeply about parents. His goal in working with parents was to teach them to organize their lives properly so they could develop the knowledge, flexibility and judgment necessary for responsible decision-making, and thoroughly enjoy the parenting process.

Essentially, Dr. Robinson's approach to child-rearing and Glasser's approach to therapy, consulting and teaching have an identical goal—that is, promoting responsible behavior. Both also realized that in order to grow into responsible adults, children need to develop self-discipline. Dr. Robinson found through his clinical research that this was best achieved through a parental attitude of "judicious neglect," especially in the early stages of child-rearing.

I would be remiss in writing this chapter if I did not share my own perceptions of Dr. Robinson and his child rearing beliefs and practices. In terms of Dr. Robinson himself, I saw him as a very knowledgeable and dedicated teacher. He wanted parents to be teachers and I believe he saw his own role as primarily that of a teacher. Although he did not describe himself as a teacher, teaching was, in my opinion, his true calling. I say this after observing him as a guest lecturer in my classes at the University of Scranton. It was clear to me that, in addition to being very good at it, he truly enjoyed teaching. He frequently said he wanted parents to begin teaching "right from the nursery."

While the obvious goal of parental teaching in Dr. Robinson's opinion was to help their children grow into responsible self-disciplined adults, there were secondary benefits as well for parents. If parents did not find themselves frequently dealing with problematic behavior on the part of their children, they could more fully enjoy their children's progress and accomplishments. This is not meant to suggest any parenting experience would be free of stress or worry, but self-disciplined and responsible children and adolescents generally will experience fewer difficulties and will be better prepared to solve problems as they arise. Also, responsible parenting can bring a true sense of lasting satisfaction to parents.

What exactly was Dr. Robinson teaching the parents with whom he worked? I believe he was teaching them to understand and appreciate the normal development process. Erikson described this process as the Epigenetic Principle which states that "we develop through an unfolding of our personality in predetermined stages, and that our environment and surrounding culture influence how we progress through these stages." Dr. Robinson helped parents to be patient and to have the forbearance needed to allow the child to grow and develop without undue interference. But he was also teaching them not to reinforce negative behaviors and how to reinforce and support positive behaviors.

Dr. Robinson's approach is consistent with the principles of a theory espoused by William Glasser called control theory. Glasser developed this theory in conjunction with a physicist, Dr. William Powers. Essentially Control Theory states that our behavior is primarily motivated by our perception of what we want or need rather than exclusively by objective reality. In order to get what it is we want or need, we use whatever behavior we have at our disposal.

While it may be difficult for us to believe that negative or positive behavior patterns can be established in infancy, Glasser points out that the infant by using the only thing they know how to do (i.e. cry), they are attempting to control others. While there may be a number of reasons why infants and young children cry, Glasser refers to deliberate crying as a way of controlling others which he called angering.

I have included Glasser's comments regarding the consequences of being overly responsive to a child in the following passage. I believe it strengthens the case for "judicious neglect."

"Though mothering a child is highly satisfying, even a devoted mother will find it difficult to subordinate her needs completely to those of a demanding child. An angering child is a tyrant, and a mother's need for freedom will begin to assert itself. A good mother also recognizes that if she becomes a slave to her baby, he won't learn to take care of himself. So not long after birth, she stops letting the baby totally control her with angering. She starts giving him the message that he has to begin to consider doing some things for himself. After he is fed, loved, cleaned, and obviously tired, his mother puts him down and does not run to him when, to assert his power, he screams for her attention. Now that angering does not work, the baby is forced to begin to consider something else to fulfill the urge he feels."

"Since all human beings are by nature creative, infants included, most will create a powerful new behavior, smiling. Once they learn that it works in terms of getting what is wanted, smiling becomes a part of their behavioral repertoire. When the baby further realizes that smiling may be more effective than angering, this behavior becomes much more frequently used. Who can resist a smiling baby?"

"Once the baby has learned that there are other behaviors besides angering, through imitating and creating he begins the rapid process of adding to his behavioral system a well-organized group of powerful acting, thinking, and feeling behaviors. Almost all of these are more effective and more pleasurable than angering."

What I believe to be remarkable is that Dr. Robinson through his knowledge of human behavior, clinical research, and intuitive skills had a remarkably clear understanding of child development. Thankfully, he shared this with such many parents over his long career. He taught parents the basic principles of control theory long before the theory was formally developed. In my opinion this provides further evidence for parents and prospective parents to carefully consider Dr. Robinson's recommendations.

Before we leave this chapter I feel it is important to discuss a bit more Dr. Robinson's suggestion to parents to practice "judicious neglect" in their childrearing. He, of course, would never advocate neglecting our children. Rather, he asked parents to be judicious—using judgment rather than just instinct in relating to their children. Peck tells us that "love is not simply giving, it is judicious giving and judicious withholding as well." He continues, judicious loving "requires thoughtful and often painful decision making." When we as parents engage in injudicious loving or giving it is in response to our own needs rather than to the spiritual and emotional needs of our children. Remember Glasser's definition of responsibility: fulfilling our needs in a way that does not deprive others of fulfilling theirs. That kind of responsible parenting is exactly what Dr. Robinson advocated.

Key Points Chapter 6

Key Point #1

Dr. Robinson was a strong advocate of parents avoiding over-handling of infants and young children and pointed out the need to establish a "disciplinary atmosphere" very early in the parenting process. The underlying principle of the parenting techniques that he advocated was what he referred to as "judicious neglect."

Key Point #2

He stressed the need for parents to help their children learn good eating and sleeping habits early in infancy and to avoid coaxing and bribing children to eat. Sleeping habits should be established within the child's first three months. He felt parents should be especially careful about using foods with a high sugar content since he found children can easily become addicted to sugar. This can lead to poor nutrition and obesity.

Key Point #3

Dr. Robinson advocated positive discipline rather than shouting, hitting or other forms of punishment that would hurt our relationships with our children. Time out, correctly implemented can be very effective.

Key Point #4

He stressed the need for treating potty training as a normal process rather than being drawn into control struggles with the child.

Key Point #5

Dr. Robinson felt strongly that children need to have chores and daily responsibilities as early as age three or fpur.

Key Point #6

Dr. Robinson believed the primary goal of parenting was to help children develop self-discipline and ultimately, emotional maturity.

Key Point #7

Perhaps the most important step in raising children to be self-disciplined and responsible is for parents to model these qualities in their own behavior.

With the permission of Dr. Robinson's son, Dr. Michael Robinson - I have included in the Appendix some actual prescriptions Dr. Robinson gave to parents. I believe they clearly demonstrate his strong, ongoing commitment to parent education. He fully expected parents to follow his advice about feeding, sleeping, discipline and chores, etc. and would take them to task when they failed to do so.

Works Cited

Glasser, W. (1984). *Control theory: A new explanation of how we control our lives.* New York: Harper and Row.

7

Choices and Habits

Consistent with Dr. Robinson's and my concern about parents exerting too much external control over their children, I am presenting an overview of William Glasser's Choice Theory and some brief excerpts from Steven Covey's *Seven Habits of Highly Effective People*. If our children are to grow into adults who can solve problems and consistently make responsible choices, Glasser and Covey tell us they need the opportunities to learn to develop a sense of inner control and to accept responsibility for the choices they make. Giving children more opportunities to respond to inner, rather than external, control can be difficult and downright scary at times. I would encourage you to try to keep an open mind to the material presented in this chapter.

Choice Theory

Before his death in 2013 at the age of eighty-eight, Dr. William Glasser published more than two dozen books promoting his view that mental health is mostly a matter of personal choice, a precept that found a vast popular audience and influenced mental health professionals, drug and alcohol counselors and teachers. His first book, which I made reference to in the introduction and in Chapter

1, "Reality Therapy" was published in 1965. His most recent work, *Choice Theory: A New Psychology of Personal Freedom*, was published in 1998. All of his writings stressed the basic tenet that in order to resolve emotional and mental problems individuals had to accept responsibility for them. By avoiding the urge to blame others, or to relive past hurts, he asserted, people could find happiness essentially by choosing behaviors that improved their relationships and increased their chances for happiness.

He describes, "Choice theory explains that, for all practical purposes, we choose everything we do, including the misery we feel. Other people can neither make us miserable nor make us happy." Further, "Choice theory teaches us we are more in control of our lives than we realize [...] For example, you choose to feel upset with your child, then you choose to yell and thereafter, things get worse, not better. Taking more effective control means making better choices as you relate to your children and everyone else."

Choice theory is a theory based on internal rather than external controls and the belief that we are internally rather than externally motivated. Glasser addressed the relationship between control and behavior in his book *Stations of the Mind* in 1981. The views he presented there were based primarily upon the work of a physicist, William Powers. Essentially Glasser pointed out that there is substantial evidence that our behaviors are motivated by our perceptions rather than being controlled by external factors. Control Theory states that, "our behavior is our constant attempt to Control our Perceptions." This is in sharp contrast to more traditional stimulus-response psychology.

As human beings we are always "controlling" for something. What we are controlling for is determined by our perception of what we want or need. Glasser continues, "First of all, no one, can actually know what goes on inside your head." In order to influence or change another's behavior we need to find out what he/she is controlling for. This is true for us as spouses and also as parents and requires on our part, the willingness to listen and be open to what we might hear, particularly when dealing with our children.

Glasser felt that most of us believe that behavior is externally controlled. He cites three beliefs of external control which influence the thinking and behaviors of the majority of people.

"*First Belief.* I answer a ringing phone, open the door to a doorbell, stop at a red light, or do countless other things because I am responding to a simple external signal.

Second Belief. I can make other people do what I want them to do even if they don't want to do it. And other people can control how I think, act, and feel.

Third Belief. It is my right, even my moral obligation, to ridicule, threaten or punish those who don't do what I tell them to do or even reward them if it will get them to do what I want."

He believed the second and third beliefs to be very harmful to human relationships. In regard to the first belief Glasser clearly points out that we answer the phone because we choose to. We can also choose not to answer: "In belief numbers two and three, the control is clearly outside the behaving person. The third belief is firmly held by many parents who believe it is their right or duty to punish, threaten, or bribe children who disobey them because it would be in their children's best interest to do as they are told."

Essentially, choice theory tells us all that we can control is our own behavior. Parents in particular have difficulty accepting this because they feel they should be able to directly control their children's behavior. Glasser points out, "They are limited to controlling their own behavior. All they can give to other people, including their children, parents and mates, is information." Information may take many forms, but information is not control. Glasser believed many people have a sense of "ownership" and believe they have the right to control their spouses and children. Glasser believed that in our attempts to control others we run the risk of harming our relationships with them. "The choice theory child-rearing axiom is this: don't choose to do anything with a child whom you want to grow up to be happy, successful and close to you, that you believe will increase the distance between you."

The acceptance of the belief that we choose everything we do and that we are not controlled externally and conversely cannot directly control others can, in my opinion, be ultimately very helpful to us as individuals and particularly, as parents.

Since choice theory is based on internal rather than external control, obviously, the first challenge for parents is to recognize and accept the fact that they cannot directly control their children and all they really can control is their own behavior. Glasser is not suggesting that we abdicate our responsibility as parents and let our kids do whatever they want. Rather, he believes parents have to learn their limitations and do as much as they can within these limitations. He offers some specific suggestions for parents:

"If you offer advice, don't repeat yourself or nag."

"Don't bring up past mistakes or failures, however, bringing up past successes may be an excellent idea."

"Let them flounder when they're young, when the penalties associated with floundering are not as severe as later."

"The basis of a choice theory relationship is trust."

"Punishment and external control always increase the distance between parents and children."

Instead of punishment, the choice theory parent sends this message: "I want you to learn from your mistakes. My job, if either of us is dissatisfied with what you choose is to get together and help you figure out a better way."

"Don't connect love with any specific behavior. Make it clear you love them no matter what they do."

"Ask yourself if I do this or say this will we be closer or farther apart. The relationship takes precedence over always being right."

"Decisions regarding attending school, health, and safety are not negotiable."

Punishment in Glasser's view is seen as doing things that will harm your relationship with your children. Choice theory requires us to recognize and accept what it is we can and cannot control.

If we choose to become "choice theory parents," we can also actively teach our children choice theory. This has been done very effectively in families and schools as reported in research at the Glasser Institute. The challenge to becoming a choice theory parent is to accept the limitations inherent in recognizing that external control does not work in the long run and that using it will likely increase the distance between you and your children. This will require us to be "emotionally intelligent" and creative and to discern accurately our responsibilities and those of our children.

I used to tell parents that all we have the right to hope for with our children is that they find success and happiness. I added that it would be up to them to decide how they would find this success and happiness. I am reminded of an occasion where I was more externally focused than choice theory oriented. My daughter, who was a senior in high school was seeking advice regarding her college major. Responding from my point of view, I noted that she was good in Math and had very good Math SAT scores. I told her that Computer Science was an area where she would probably do well and get a good job. She took my advice and majored in Computer Science. She came home after the first semester and told me she was not happy with her choice of a major. Although her grades were good, she did not see this as being a good choice for her. At that point, I did what I should have done in the first place—asking her what her values, ideals and goals were, what made her feel happy and proud and how she wanted to see herself in ten years. She thought about these questions and changed her major to Education. Fortunately, she has had a very successful career in education. Thankfully, we sometimes get a second chance as parents. In addition to success and happiness, we might strive for maintaining positive relationships with them. Fortunately, my late wife and I enjoyed positive ongoing relationships with our three children although they all reside out of the area in which they grew up. An added bonus is, as a result, we also have very positive relationships with our grandchildren. This is a great source of joy for us, increasingly so as we have grown older.

This is not to say that we never made mistakes as parents with our children, but apparently we were somehow able to communicate to them how much we valued them and our relationships with them.

The Seven Habits

The belief that we are internally rather than externally controlled was also present in the work of Steven Covey. In his highly successful book, *The Seven Habits of Highly Effective People*, he points out that responsibility is really two words, response and ability. Human beings, unlike laboratory animals, do not have to respond automatically to stimuli but have a *choice* between stimulus and response and can respond in a variety of ways. Covey reviewed two hundred years of success literature. He found that the most valid works were written in the first one hundred and fifty years. More recent literature tended to be superficial and manipulative while the earlier works focused on what he called the *Character Ethic* as the real foundation for success. He noted successful living and parenting requires us to be principle centered rather than relying upon techniques or gimmicks. He listed, "integrity, humility, fidelity, temperance, courage, justice, patience, industry, simplicity, modesty and the Golden Rule" as characteristics of principle centered people. If parents are principle centered, they can be proactive rather than reactive in their dealings with their children. They can rely on these principles to evaluate what is happening to them and their children and choose how to respond.

As noted above, after reviewing the success literature, Covey concluded that success literature could be roughly divided into two groups or schools of thought, those that stressed what he referred to as the Character Ethic and those that stressed the Personality Ethic.

In the Personality Ethic, according to Covey, "Success became a function of personality, of public image, of attitudes and behaviors, skills, and techniques that lubricate the processes of human interaction." He continued, "Other parts of the personality approach were clearly manipulative, even deceptive, encouraging people to use techniques to get other people to like them ... or to intimidate their way through life." On the other hand, the character Ethic taught "that these are basic principles of effective living, and that people can only experience true success and enduring happiness as they learn to integrate these principles into their basic character."

Covey identifies seven habits of highly effective people. All of these habits can be applied to parenting. In order to be consistently responsible and effective as parents we need to be principle centered and develop habits that will enable us to act on these principles. Parenting must be viewed as a developmental process rather than just a set of techniques. We also need to help our children become principle centered through our modeling these characteristics and through our day-to-day interactions with them.

Covey defined a habit as the intersection of knowledge, skill and desire. Parents need to know what to, why to, how to, and they must work to internalize these principles and patterns of effective behavior.

A full discussion of Covey's "7 Habits" is beyond the scope of this book. Covey discusses each in great detail and offers examples and exercises to help readers better understand and incorporate these habits into their daily lives. I strongly encourage any parents or prospective parents to become familiar with Covey's work. All of the Habits incorporate Covey's belief that in order to be successful as individuals (and parents) we need to accept full responsibility for our behavior and our decisions and base these behaviors and decisions on our internal value systems rather than being "driven by feelings, by circumstances, by conditions or their environments." He also recommends developing personal mission statements and carefully prioritizing "our day to day activities in a way that truly reflect our values, goals and ideals as parents." Covey also offers invaluable insights regarding communication and conflict resolution. Covey's final Habit "Sharpening the Saw" notes the importance of taking the time to take care of ourselves, physically, mentally, spiritually and emotionally and to encourage our children and create opportunities for them to do likewise. A very Brief overview of the seven habits follows:

Habit 1: Be Proactive- Covey defined proactivity as "meaning more than merely taking initiative. It means that as human beings, we are responsible for our own lives. He continues, "The ability to subordinate an impulse to a value is the essence of the proactive person. Reactive people are driven by feelings, by circumstances, by conditions, by their environments. Proactive people are driven by value – carefully thought about selected and internalized value."

Habit 2: Begin with the End in Mind- "Begin with the end in mind is based on the principle that all things are created twice. There's a mental first creation, and a physical or second creation to all things." As human beings we have the capacity to write our own script. Fundamentally, "Habit 2 is based on principles of personal leadership, which means that leadership is the first creation". Parents, whether they like it or not, are placed in the position of leadership in the family system. Accepting this position requires asking ourselves what do I want to accomplish as a parent? This book is written on the assumption that most parents would value having responsible children. Covey recommends developing a personal mission statement as the most effective way to begin with the end in mind. He describes this as a statement of one's philosophy or creed as well as what we are trying to achieve. While the task of writing a personal mission statement might seem a bit academic or contrived, I believe the exercise is well worth the effort.

Habit 3: Put First Things First- All of us have a number of roles which we attempt to carry out to the best of our ability. Most parents would put family as their first priority and I am sure that the fact that you are reading this book would put you in that category. However, Covey found in a number of extensive surveys (including over a quarter of a million people) that "Habit 3, is, of all the habits, the one where people consistently give themselves the lowest marks." Most people feel there is a real gap between what really matters most to them, including family, and the way they lead their daily lives: "Often parenting and family are subordinated to a number of other activities and relationships. In order to function at high levels of effectiveness as individuals and parents, we need to find a way to prioritize our day to day activities in a way that truly reflect our values, goals and ideals as parents."

Habit 4: Think Win Win- All human behavior, by definition, has the potential for conflict and can at times be adversarial. Conflicts between parent and child are no exception. Given their position of leadership in the family, parents need to find ways of resolving conflicts with our children that enable both of us to "win." To accomplish this, Covey believes we need "a frame of mind and heart that constantly seeks mutual benefits in all human interactions."

Habit 5: Seek First to Understand, then to be Understood - This habit is based on the work of clinicians and communication experts who have discovered a very powerful communication technique called empathetic understanding or active listening. Carl Rogers in his seminal work *Client Centered Therapy* stressed the potential effectiveness of empathetic understanding in therapeutic relationships. Others, including Thomas Gordon and Haim Ginott, have advocated incorporating these techniques into the parenting process. Covey noted that "Communication is the most important skill in life." Good communication is necessary for establishing and maintaining relationships as well as resolving problems and conflicts.

Habit 6: Synergize: Covey considered synergy as "the essence of principle entered behavior." Essentially this concept is taken from General Systems Theory and is referred to as "non-summatority." That is, the whole is greater than the sum of its parts. Synergizing involves incorporating all of the other habits into a working whole. Covey notes, "When you communicate synergistically, you are simply opening your mind and head and expressions to new persons, to new personalities, new alternatives, new options."

Habit 7: Sharpening the Saw- As previously noted, this habit recognizes the importance of taking the time to take care of yourself, physically mentally, spiritually, socially and emotionally. As parents we also need to encourage our children and create opportunities for them to do likewise. Acting as role models in this regard can have a powerful influence on our children. Covey states we need to realize the importance of preserving and enhancing the greatest asset we have – ourselves.

Glasser's Control Theory and Covey's "Seven Habits" were presented to underscore my belief and that of Dr. Robinson that effective parenting can only take place when parents accept full responsibility for their behavior. We can only be responsible for what we can control and all that we can control is our own behavior. As Glasser notes it is often our attempt to control others that harm our relationships with them. It is only when we have a positive relationship with our children that we can provide information which we believe would be helpful to them. Covey's work emphasizes the importance of having clearly defined values, beliefs, principles, and ways of acting in accord with these values, beliefs and principles.

I truly believe although Dr. Robinson may not have been aware of Glaser's Choice Theory or Covey's work, he would have agreed with their emphasis on behavior being internally motivated. His recommendations to parents would help them to provide the structure and appropriate level of guidance needed for their children to become self-directed and to have the self-discipline necessary for making responsible choices.

Key Points Chapter 7

Key Point #1

Choice Theory is based on internal rather than external control. This is a difficult concept for many parents to conceptualize and accept. Most of us grew up in a world that focused on external control and motivation. Using that frame of reference, it was logical to affix blame or fault for any of our difficulties on factors outside of our control. It may also be difficult to accept our lack of control over others. Especially those that we care about the most. If we can accept the belief that behavior is motivated by internal rather than external factors, we can focus on what we can control (our behavior and our relationships with our children).

Key Point #2

Glasser defines punishment as anything that will harm your relationship with your children. Punishment should not be confused with discipline. Remember one of the desired outcomes of parenting is having our children learn self-discipline. They are much more likely to do so if they learn how to choose rather than if all their choices are made for them.

Key Point #3

Corey also states that we are internally rather than externally motivated. He points out the advantages of being proactive and beginning with the end in mind. I have found his comments regarding prioritizing, communicating and resolving conflicts to be very helpful in working with parents.

Key Point #4

By practicing choice theory principles, we are also teaching our children these principles which I believe will be helpful to them in numerous ways throughout their lives.

Key Point #5

Allowing our children to make choices when it is appropriate to do so requires great courage and patience on the part of parents.

Works Cited

Covey, S. (1989). *The Seven Habits of Highly Effective People.* New York, NY: Simon & Schuster.

Glasser, W. (1981). *Stations of the Mind.* New York, NY: Harper & Row.

Glasser, W. (1998). *Choice Theory: A New Psychology of Personal Freedom.* New York, NY: Harper & Row.

8

Overparenting and How To Avoid It

Dr. Robinson's recommendations to parents that they approach child rearing with an attitude of *judicious neglect* was the result of his findings from meticulous research. In his over ten years of collecting and analyzing information from parents, he saw how overhandling and failure to establish good eating and sleeping patterns could lead to children developing bad habits, overdependence, and problematic behaviors. He saw how these bad habits and problems could be very difficult to reverse later on. He found that parents need to establish what he referred to as a *disciplinary atmosphere* very early in the parenting process in order for their children to learn self-discipline. He also saw how being overly protective of children and not teaching them how to solve problems failed to prepare them for success in school or other developmental challenges. He of course, worked primarily with young children and adolescents and was not able to conduct longitudinal studies to determine how all his former patients functioned as adults. However, it appears that many of his concerns regarding the consequences of overparenting have come to bear, particularly in the current population of late adolescents and young adults.

The phenomenon of overparenting has been a cause for concern by an increasing number of those involved in the education, treatment, and direction of children, adolescents, and young adults. Julie Lythcott-Haines, a former dean at Stanford University notes this concern in her recent book, *How to Raise an Adult*, an excellent discussion of overparenting and ways to escape what she referred to as the "overparenting trap." She asks parents to become aware of how harmful overparenting is to children, parents, and society in general. Essentially, this harm results when we do too much for our kids. I have often cautioned parents against doing things for their children that they can do for themselves!

In her work in the later 1990s as a dean at Stanford, Lythcott-Haines began to notice, as did her Stanford colleagues, "A new phenomenon- parents on the college campus, virtually and literally. Each subsequent year would bring an increase in the number of parents who did things like seek opportunities, make decisions, and problem solve for their sons and daughters—things that college-aged students used to be able to do for themselves." Conversations with colleagues at other colleges and universities indicated this was a nationwide phenomenon.

Looking at short term results, Lythcott-Haines noted this over-involvement in their children's lives can result in "short-term gains in the forms of safer opportunities attained and outcomes secured." However, she questions whether this over-involvement can do psychological harm. "And did some of these parents go so far in the direction of their own wants and needs that they eclipsed their own kids' chances to develop a critical psychological trait called "self-efficacy?"

Lythcott-Haines states this overparenting can stem from our love of our kids but also appears to be the result of our fears. She comments on the results of her extensive research on the topic of overparenting: "But in my years researching this book I've learned that many of our behaviors stem from fears, perhaps chief among them is the fear that our kids won't be successful out in the world" She continues, "Of course, it's natural for parents to want their kids to succeed, but based on research, interviews with more than a hundred people, and my own personal experiences, I've come to the conclusion that we define our success too narrowly."

In analyzing when, why, and how parenting in our society has shifted from previous beliefs that children should be seen and not heard and the parental retort, because I said so to over handling infants and toddlers and hovering over our kids like "helicopters," Lythcott-Haines looked at a number of factors occurring primarily in the 1980's when the so called "Baby Boomers" began parenting.

She explains, "One such shift arose from the increased awareness of child abductions." This received extensive media coverage and led to made for TV movies, books, and a television series. Some very positive outcomes resulted. Congress created a National Center for Missing and Exploited Children in 1984 and other protection laws were passed. However, this increased awareness led to many parents becoming overly fearful and restrictive of their children.

Additionally, "another shift- the idea that our children aren't doing enough schoolwork- arrived with the publication of *A Nation at Risk* in 1983 which argued that American children weren't competing well against their peers globally." This shift has contributed to programs like No Child Left Behind and Race to the Top. These programs, while well intentioned, have led to increased emphasis on rote memorization and teaching to the test. Many noteworthy educational professionals have questioned the wisdom of this emphasis. One very obvious outcome of this increased emphasis on achievement has been increased schoolwork, often to an overwhelming level for achievement-oriented students (and in many cases their parents). Studies indicate an increasing number of parents who supervise and check their kids' homework and, in many cases, actually do the homework and projects to ensure good grades.

Further, "a third shift came from the self-esteem movement." This led to initiatives like Affective Education and an emphasis upon helping kids express their feelings and feel good about themselves. I personally believe there were positive outcomes from this movement, particularly for children who were emotionally at risk. However, I also saw examples of excesses which led to a preoccupation with ensuring our kids' happiness and emotional well-being by protecting them from experiencing any frustration or failure.

The fourth shift was the creation of the play date. In regards to the play date, Lythcott-Haines notes, "once parents began scheduling play, they began observing play, which led to involving themselves in play, leaving kids home alone became taboo, as did allowing kids to play unsupervised." She continues, "The very nature of play, which is a foundational element in the life of a developing child, begins to change."

The self-esteem movement in its attempt to protect children's feelings gave rise to the Everyone gets a trophy. Children were given recognition, including badges and trophies for merely participating in sports or other events. Lythcott-Haines notes the danger of fostering in children a "belief in entitlement, a recognition and promotion that will dog them in the workplace years later." She makes reference to the work of Amanda Ripley, author of the 2013 book, *The Smartest Kids in the World* who, in commenting on America's poor ranking on international standardized tests, noted "America's parents and teachers had been bombarded with claims that children's self-esteem needed to be protected from competition (and reality) in order for them to succeed."

Psychologist Wendy Mogel writes of learning through trial and error in *The Blessing of the Skinned Knee*. She notes that many modern parents "seem to have equated 'good' or 'successful' parenting with ensuring our kids never experience even minor, short time pain." While I agree the negative effects of overparenting may cause numerous problems for children, parents, and society in general, I have been more specifically focused on the psychological harm done. In order to move successfully through childhood, adolescence, and into adulthood, I believe we need to develop a psychological trait identified by the psychologist Albert Bandura as "self-efficacy." This is defined as "the belief in one's capabilities to organize and execute the courses of action required to manage prospective situations." That is, we need to develop a belief in ourselves and our ability to face challenges. Overparenting causes many children and adolescents to grow into adults lacking this sense of self-efficacy.

Numerous studies indicate significant emotional problems experienced by college students. For example, a study conducted by the American College Health Association surveyed close to 100,000 students from one hundred and fifty-three different campuses about their health. When asked about their experiences, at some point over the past twelve months, a very high percentage felt overwhelmed by all they had to and exhausted (but not from physical activity). In addition, 60.5% felt very sad, 57% felt very lonely, and 51.3% felt overwhelming anxiety. 46.5% felt things were hopeless, 38.8% felt overwhelming anger, and 31.7% felt so depressed that it was difficult to function.

This obvious conclusion Lythcott-Haines comes to is that far too many parents, including herself, have been overprotective, overdirecting, and overinvolved in the lives of their kids. She asks, "Why did parenting change from preparing our kids for life to protecting them from life?" She further notes that she understands that overparenting stems from our worries about our kids being successful, but we need to find the courage to change.

As you've probably surmised by now, the underlying theme of this book is meant to be consistent with Dr. Robinson's philosophy of *judicious neglect*. He believed overparenting began as he put, 'in the nursery." He advocated parents finding a way to maintain responsibility for their kids that did not deprive children of the opportunity to learn and practice responsible behavior. I believe he would agree with and heartily endorse Lythcott-Haines's observations. She continues, "For our kids' sakes, and also our own, we need to stop parenting from fear and bring a more healthy—a more widely loving—approach back into our communities, schools, and homes."

Obviously in order to follow her advice, many parents would have to change. As Peck has told us, change can be quite painful and must begin with a thorough and honest self-examination. Following this self-evaluation, it may do well to remind ourselves that as sociologist Jim Hancock points out- if we think we're raising children, then what we'll have in the end is children. He advises us to define our tasks as raising adults. But what does it mean to be an adult?

Lythcott-Haines cites a 2007 study published in the *Journal of Family Psychology* which asked eighteen to twenty-five year olds which criteria they felt were most indicative of adulthood: "Their criteria were, in order of importance: 1. Accepting responsibility for the consequences of your actions. 2. Establishing a relationship with parents as an equal adult. 3. Being financially independent from parents, and 4. Deciding on beliefs/values independently of parents/other influences." The researchers then asked these young adults, "Do you think that you have reached adulthood? And only 16% said yes." Parents of these young adults were asked the same question, and they overwhelmingly agreed with their children. Lythcott-Haines adds, "Based on my observations of close to twenty thousand 18 to 22 year olds in my time as dean, I concur and I find it problematic." She sees this situation as parenting failure and notes, "Kids don't acquire life skills by magic at the stroke of midnight on their eighteenth birthday. When we haven't prepared our children—and ourselves—for the inevitable day when they'll have to fend for themselves, it will be a rude awakening for both."

Dr. Robinson told me on a number of occasions that he had

to work hard with parents to get them to not interfere with their children's learning skills they would need as adults. Several studies indicate an increase in mental health problems among college students. Significant differences were found among students with "helicopter" parents and those who were given more responsibility for their own wellbeing. The latter group, so called "free rangers," had fewer symptoms and were less likely to be medicated for anxiety and depression. Other studies have found students with helicopter parents to express less satisfaction in life and less executive function capabilities. Lythcott-Haines explains, "Executive function is our ability to determine which goal directed actions to carry out and when and is a skill set lacking in many kids with ADHD/ADD." Other research suggests that college students with poor life skills are more likely to become involved with drugs, alcohol, gambling, or self-mutilation.

Lythcott-Haines notes the concerns expressed to her by a staff psychologist in a large university counseling center regarding students who have not learned to struggle and have not experienced failure. They can develop a fear of failure and letting others down. Both of which can lead to poor self-esteem and a number of psychological symptoms. Lythcott-Haines further cites the work of child development researchers Foster Cline and Jim Fay who, in 1990, coined the term "helicopter parents" to refer to a parent "who hovers over a child in a way that runs counter to the parent's responsibility to raise a child to independence." A 2013 study of two hundred ninety seven college students found that children with helicopter parents reported significantly higher levels of depression and less satisfaction in life and attributed this diminishment of well-being to a situation of the students' "basic psychological need for autonomy and competence." A 2014 study at the University of Colorado was the first to correlate "a highly structured childhood with less executive function capabilities."

What kinds of overparenting styles lead to psychological harm?

Dr. Madeline Levone, a psychologist from California identifies three ways in which overparenting can cause psychological harm: "1. When we do for our kids what they can *already* do for themselves. 2. When we do for our kids what they can *almost* do for themselves. 3. When our parenting behavior is motivated by our own needs."

Dr. Levone concluded that when we parent this way, we "deprive our kids of the opportunity to be creative, to problem solve, to develop coping skills, to build resilience, to figure out what makes them happy, to figure out who they are."

At this point hopefully having convinced those reading this book of the dangers of overparenting, what kind of parenting style would be most likely to provide effective leadership but avoid overparenting? Lythcott-Haines discusses this issue by presenting four parental types.

Parental Types

Psychologist Eleanor Maccoby and John Marin modified earlier work by a developmental psychologist Diana Bajem which identified four parenting types. These four types have been accepted as definitive by developmental psychologists:

1. *Authoritarian-* these parents are characterized as demanding and unresponsive. They expect obedience and respect and punish their children for failing to comply. They don't explain the reason for their actions. They value achievement, order, discipline, and self-control.
2. *Permissive/Indulgent-* these parents are characterized as undemanding and responsive. They tend to attend to their child's every need and comply with their child's every request. They are reluctant to establish rules of expectation and have little need for discipline. They remind to the point

of nagging, but do not follow through with consequences. They give in frequently and have trouble saying no.
3. *Neglectful-* these parents are characterized as undemanding and unresponsive. These parents are, at best "hands off" and at worst criminally negligent. They are underinvolved in their child's school and home life and are emotionally distant and often physically absent. They may be unreliable in providing basic necessities for their children.
4. *Authoritative-* these parents are characterized as demanding and responsive. They set high standards, expectations, and limits which they uphold with consequences. They are also emotionally warm, and responsive to the child's emotional needs. They give their children freedom to explore, to fail, and to make their own choices.

Obviously, the authoritative parent would be the least likely to be caught in the "overparenting trap" as Lythcott-Haines terms it. Examining our parenting approach on a regular basis and striving for authoritative parenting is highly recommended.

For parents who would like to learn more about what specific life skills kids should have at the various levels of development, the *Family Education Network* is an excellent resource. This site was founded in 1996 and claims to be the oldest site for parenting on the Web. A 2012 article by Lindsay Hutton, the associate editor of the network specifically outlines living skills by category. Hopefully this will be helpful as a starting point for setting expectations." (Please note: a request has been submitted to the Family Life Education Network to include this information.)

Ages 2-3: Small Chores and Basic Grooming

By the age of three, your child should be able to:

Help put his toys away
Dress himself (with some help form you)
Put his clothes in the hamper when he undresses
Clean up his plate after meals
Assist in setting the table
Brush his teeth and wash his face with assistance

Ages 4 to 5: Important Names and Numbers

When your child reaches this age, safety skills are high on the list. She should:

Know her full name, address, and phone number
Know how to make an emergency call

She should be able to:

Perform simple chores such as dusting in easy to reach places and cleaning the table after meals
Feed pets
Identify monetary denominations, and understand the very basic concept of how money is used
Brush her teeth, comb her hair, and wash her face without assistance
Help with basic laundry chores, such as putting her clothes away and bringing her dirty clothes to the laundry area.
Choose her own clothes to wear

Ages 6 to 7: Basic Cooking Techniques

Kids at this age can start to help with cooking meals and learn to:

- Mix, stir, and cut with a knife
- Make a basic meal, such as a sandwich
- Help put the groceries away
- Wash the dishes
- Use basic household cleaners safely
- Make his bed without assistance
- Bathe unsupervised

Ages 8 to 9: Pride in Personal Belongings

- Fold her clothes
- Learning simple sewing
- Care for outdoor toys
- Take care of personal choices without being told to do so
- Use a broom and dustpan properly
- Read a recipe and prepare a simple meal
- Help create a grocery list
- Count and make change
- Take written phone messages
- Take out the trash

Ages 10 to 13: Gaining Independence

Ten is about the age when your child should be able to perform many skills independently. He should know how to:

   Stay home alone
   Go to the store and make purchases for himself
   Change his own bedsheets
   Use the washing machine and dryer
   Plan and prepare a meal with served ingredients
   Use the oven to broil or bake goods
   Read labels
   Iron his clothes
   Learn to use hand tools
   Mow the lawn
   Look after younger siblings or neighbors

Ages 14 to 18: More advanced skills are learned

Your child should have a very good mastering of all previous skills. On top of that, she should be able to:

   Prepare more sophisticated cleaning and maintenance chores
   Fill a car with gas, add air, and change tire
   Read and understand medicine labels
   Interview for and get a job
   Prepare and cook meals

Young Adults: Preparing to Live on His Own

Your child will need to know how to support himself when he goes away to college or moves out. These are still a few skills he should know before venturing out on his own including:

> Make regular doctor and dentist appointments and other health related appointments
> Have a basic understanding of finances, manage his bank account, balance a checkbook, pay a bill, and use a credit card
> Understand basic contexts like an apartment or lease
> Schedule oil changes and basic car maintenance

This list may seem daunting and you may conclude that you've done too much for your kids if your kids are grown up, but for those of you who aren't at this stage, consider this list carefully. Remember by being overly helpful you are depriving your children from experiencing the joy of doing thigs on their own.

Obviously, overparenting as all of our behaviors, does not occur in a vacuum. If we choose to avoid the overparenting trap, we need to be aware of the many variables which affect and influence the parenting process. There undoubtedly will be challenges both from without and within the multigenerational family system. Appropriate boundary setting, and maintenance, and ongoing awareness of the fact that we are given the task as parents of transforming our children into capable, responsible adults will be necessary at all stages of parenting.

Key Points Chapter #8

Key Point #1

There is considerable evidence from multiple sources to indicate that overparenting interferes with the developmental steps naturally built into childhood through which children acquire competence and independence.

Key Point #2

Setting narrow goals for our children and over concern regarding their accomplishment of these goals can be quite harmful to them.

Key Point #3

Children need the opportunity to learn how to deal with frustration and failure on their own to develop psychological resiliency and self-confidence.

Key Point #4

When we do things for our children they can (or almost can) for themselves, we are likely responding to our needs rather than theirs.

Key Point #5

Overparenting often begins with overhanding infants and young children.

Key Point #6

Remember the importance of play.

Key Point #7

Consider that the cell phone has been called the "world's largest umbilical cord."

Key Point #8

Children need to experience life rather than constantly being protected from it.

Key Point #9

Which of the four parental types best characterizes you? Your parenting partners?

Key Point #10

Review the specific living skills categories and see which you can incorporate into your parenting.

Works Cited

American College Health Association. "Emotional Problem Experienced by College Students" cited in Lythcott-Haines *How to Raise an Adult*.

Bandura, A. *Self Efficacy* cited in Lythcott-Haines *How to Raise an Adult*.

Cline, F. & Fay, J. "Helicopter Parents" cited in Lythcott-Haines *How to Raise an Adult.*

Journal of Family Psychology. "Criteria for Adulthood" cited in Lythcott-Haines *How to Raise an Adult.*

Lythcott-Haines, J. (2015). *How to Raise an Adult.* New York, NY: Henry Holt & Company.

Mogel, W. *The Blessing of the Skinned Knee* cited in Lythcott-Haines *How to Raise an Adult.*

Levone, M. *Overparenting* cited in Lythcott-Haines *How to Raise an Adult.*

Macohy, E. & Marin, J. "Parental Types" cited in Lythcott-Haines *How to Raise an Adult.*

9

Additional Considerations and Observations

Single Parenting

I believe all of the fundamental principles of responsible parenting apply to single parents as well. Obviously "going it alone" can and does present a number of additional challenges. I believe the first challenge is similar to one previously noted in this book, that is, acknowledging the inherent difficulties one might face as a single parent. In studying Buddhism, Scott Peck emphasized Buddha's "Noble Truths." Buddha's first truth, "Life is suffering," Peck paraphrased as: "Life is *difficult*." Both parenting and in particular single parenting are difficult. Buddha and Peck believed that if we accept this fact, life (and parenting) will be less difficult. I believe single parents also need to acknowledge the differences between their situations and two parent families. I have found that many single parents consciously or unconsciously deny the differences and by so doing create further difficulties for themselves and their children. Acceptance of the difficulties and differences is challenging but I believe it is the crucial first step toward responsible single parenting.

This acceptance will help alleviate much of the guilt many single parents experience because they feel their children have been deprived of a more "normal" family experience. Guilt and competency are inversely related and excessive guilt can lead to exaggerated efforts and overcompensations to "make up" for the absence of a parenting partner. This almost always leads to less than responsible parenting.

In reality, most single parents are not really all alone. Very often they receive significant help from their family of origin and a variety of other sources. They need to be assertive and resourceful in seeking other sources of support. When sharing some of the parenting with relatives, friends, etc., it is important to establish and maintain appropriate boundaries and effective communication. Speaking of boundaries, it may be more difficult in a single parent family to maintain appropriate generational boundaries. However, it remains very important to do so. Any sharing of responsibilities with others should be carefully negotiated and evaluated on an ongoing basis. Most single parents find it very helpful to encourage their children to participate in activities such as team sports, boys' and girls' clubs, YMCAs. Children can find very positive role models and support from the adults who coach or supervise these activities.

Divorce and Remarriage

Michael Nichols, a psychologist and family therapist in his book, *The Power of the Family* addressed divorce, primarily from a family systems perspective. He noted, "Much of the trouble in many divorces is due to a blurring of the distinction between martial and parental subsystems. "Ex" and "former" refer to the martial relationships, not the parental one. Letting go of the former means getting past anger and giving up secret hope for reunion." He continues, "Divorce is not an ending, it is a transition. In divorce, the family must change the nature of its boundaries, establishing a firm separation between husband and wife, but permitting access to both parents—by the children, and each other."

He further remarks, "Divorce can be a creative attempt of family members to develop a new shape. For husbands and wives and children, divorce may be a loss and liberation. For the family, it is the transformation from an old pattern into a new one. The family system has to maintain some subsystems, shed others, and develop new ones. Boundaries between couples must be strengthened to facilitate the individuation of the divorced spouses, boundaries between both parents and the children must be kept open enough to allow contact, and new relationships will require further complex boundary-making". "In short, parents need to let go of each other as spouses, and the family system needs to let go of its former structure in order to establish a new one."

As I earlier noted, I have done my share of marital therapy. When couples could not resolve their differences, separation and divorce sometimes resulted. I worked with ex-spouses to help them to deal with the pain and suffering associated with divorce and to go through a process of mourning and grieving not only the loss of the marriage but also the loss of their emotional investment in the marriage. This can be a long and difficult process, but it is absolutely necessary to continuing to be responsible parents.

Extensive longitudinal research on children whose parents divorce vs those in intact families has found that many of the former group do as well if not better than the latter group. In my own experience, I have found that in some instances, children may become the battle ground for unresolved marital problems. This places a great deal of stress upon them. If parents cannot find a way to resolve their problems, it may be much better for children if the parents do separate. When this happens, the parents need to maturely and responsibly deal with custody issues and ongoing communication with their ex-spouses.

Unfortunately, some of the most contentious situations I have dealt with professionally were custody disputes. In addition to the problems these disputes can present for the ex-spouses, the children may also suffer significant emotional damage. If you should find yourself in such a situation, I suggest you reread earlier chapters of this book and seek professional help.

Often divorce can lead to remarriage or significant relationships with another single parent. This may create challenges in establishing and maintaining functional "blended" families. All of the basic principles of responsible parenting apply to stepparents as well. I am a strong believer that in the process of "blending", help from a family therapist or counselor can be crucial, especially early on in the process. Even if there are no apparent problems, the counseling can help to prevent future difficulties.

Nichols notes that "both nurturing and limit setting can present difficulties for stepparents due to the lack of a natural sequence found in biological families. Many established patterns of parenting and interacting as a family may have to be evaluated and, where possible, modified. To do so requires emotional maturity and a careful evaluation of the structure and communication of the overall family system and the various subsystems."

Differences

Although the title of this Book is Raising Responsible Kids you will notice that the vast majority of the discussion has been focused on parents rather than on kids. One might assume from this that I believe all children are alike and there is only one way to parent every child. Nothing could be further from the truth. Children differ from day one in a number of significant ways. Their temperament, personality, activity level and tolerance for frustration can differ greatly. Children also differ in the ways they think, perceive and respond emotionally. The most important thing for parents to remember is that every child is uniquely different. The challenge to us is to recognize these differences and respond in ways that will help our children maximize their potential. The statement that every child is different may sound a bit cliché. However, there is no doubt in my mind that it is true. Perhaps two of my most fascinating and enlightening therapeutic experiences came from working with two families with identical twins (both girls). When I was really able to get to know the girls individually, I was amazed at how different they were in a number of ways. Both sets of twins were seen as alike in almost every way by their parents and others. When they were able to openly express their different perceptions and opinions in family sessions, their parents were amazed as well. Interestingly in both cases, the older twin (by minutes) had all of the characteristics of the first-born child while the younger one typified the middle child (each family had a younger male child).

Obviously, some children are more challenging to parents than others for a variety of reasons. As Dr. Robinson noted, a colicky baby can present a number of difficulties regarding eating, sleeping, etc. If not handled correctly, bad habits established during these very early stages of development can have adverse long-term consequences. (Children with medical problems also present challenges in a number of ways). Children with high activity levels and low tolerance for frustration can be particularly challenging as can children with a variety of special needs, including learning problems. By the way, there is such a thing as ADHD. For unknown reasons, some children's neurological systems develop unevenly. When the so-called inhibitory system is underdeveloped, these children can be hyperactive, impulsive and, at times, aggressive. They can have marked difficulties in attending and concentrating which become particularly problematic when they enter school. In my experience, when children who clearly meet the diagnostic criteria for ADHD, are treated with the appropriate dosage of a psychostimulant, most show significant improvement in a number of domains. Addressing all of the various childhood mental disorders and their unique challenges to parents is not intended in this book but there are ample references available to parents for better understanding these problems and choosing a course of action. If you believe your child is showing any signs of developmental delays, it is important to seek help as early as possible.

Very creative children can present a number of potential challenges to parents as well. Since they tend to be divergent rather than convergent thinkers, they often see the world quite differently than their peers, parents or teachers. I have worked with highly creative children and their parents in efforts to bring about mutual understanding and acceptance of these differences. Although these children are usually very bright they may, particularly in adolescence, rebel in some ways against what they see as rigid educational demands or attempts to have them conform to various standards and rules.

One of the most dramatic case examples of the difficulties highly creative adolescents may face was a seventeen-year-old girl who was referred to me after being hospitalized following a suicide attempt. Up until shortly before being hospitalized, she had been excelling academically. She was second in her class in a large high school and, with no special preparation, scored above 1400 in her S.A.T.s. She also excelled musically and was a very gifted artist. Her parents had recently divorced and everyone (including me) saw this as the primary reason for her feelings of depression. I was able to help her reasonably well with the divorce issues but she still remained moderately depressed. She was no longer experiencing suicidal ideation and had contracted not to harm herself before we began therapy. However, she did not want to return to school. She told me she felt like a failure because of her inability to perceive things the way her peers (and siblings) did. She felt "out of place" and inferior to others. Despite my best efforts to be empathetic and affirming, she still continued to be self-deprecating and irrational in her self-appraisal. We were able to work out an arrangement with her school where she attended on a half time basis and worked part time. She was a senior and had more than enough credits to graduate. As sometimes happens in therapy (and in life), we got lucky. She had begun talking to her parish priest (a very talented musician) regarding a number of issues. He suggested she read the biographies of famous artists and musicians. She enthusiastically followed his advice and found that, in general, their adolescent thoughts, feelings, and experiences were remarkably similar to hers. This greatly helped her sense of self-esteem and she was able to optimistically plan for her future. She excelled in college and professionally and she is a happily married mother of two children. The point of this example is that often creative children, when they reach adolescence where there is so much emphasis on conforming and belonging, may see themselves as "misfits" and suffer emotionally. It is often hard for parents to be accurately empathetic and supportive. Calling upon your reservoir of emotional intelligence will be necessary and helpful in these situations.

There are a large number of other variables that may account for differences in children's behavior that parents need to be aware of and sensitive to. Sibling order can significantly influence children's attitudes and behaviors. For example, first born children are often strong willed and exhibit leadership qualities while middle children are more concerned with pacifying and helping others. Also, the rate at which children physically mature can strongly influence their adjustment. Research studies indicate that early maturing boys have the easiest adolescence while early maturing girls have the most difficult time. These examples are, of course, generalizations and may not apply in all instances. Identifying all of the factors that may influence children's behavior is beyond the scope of this book. Suffice to say there are many variables that will call for parents to identify and skillfully respond to these individual differences.

Power and Control

One of the primary issues in any human interaction is that of control. All of us would like to have some measure of control over the important variables in our lives. When we sense a loss of control, we are likely to be fearful and worrisome. Many of the symptoms associated with anxiety disorders are essentially irrational attempts at control. This issue is particularly relevant for parents. Aside from our survival needs, Glasser believed we also have a number of "non-survival" needs: Love, Belonging, Power, Freedom and Fun, along with the need for helping others and gaining recognition in our own right. Glasser believed that among our "non-survival" needs are the needs for power & control. Since we live in an external control society, as parents it is natural to exert our need for power vis-a-vis our children. Power in itself is neither good nor bad. It depends according to Glasser on "how it is defined, acquired and used that makes the difference." It was his belief that "we gain more power in trying to get along with people than in trying to dominate them."

We need to find out what our kids want and find ways to negotiate any differences with them as they arise. We also need to maintain a good relationship with our kids to continue to able to effectively discipline them. Punishments and threats don't change behavior. In Glasser's words "they (our children) remove us from their heads as need satisfying people." In short, they stop paying attention to us. Glasser's advice to parents: "Try as hard as possible to teach, show and help your children to gain effective control of their lives. Don't do things that will cause your kids to lose control. Even irresponsible behaviors are attempts by kids to regain control of their lives. If they blame us, they lose even more control."

Glasser continues, "When discipline is reasonable and understandable and when the parents' own behavior is consistent with their demands on the child, he/she will love and respect them even though his/her surface attitude may not always show it."

An excessive need for control can lead to parents being chronically worrisome and fearful. Their children are likely to incorporate these attitudes and behaviors into their own ways of thinking and acting. When reflecting on your experiences in your family of origin, do you remember your parents and/or grandparents being chronic "worriers?" Has this carried over into your parenting? I remember how I literally had to force myself not to give a list of do's and don'ts to my adolescent and young adult children before they went out for the evening. With a good deal of conscious effort, I was finally able to say *"Have a good time"* rather than lecturing about the potential dangers.

The issue of power and control is also very significant in the realm of marital relations. The primary reason why I have encouraged the exploration of our families of origin is that many control struggles stem from spouses struggling to determine whose family of origin will our family more closely resemble? Often this struggle is at a less than conscious level, however, I found it to be present in virtually all of the families I worked with in therapy. The issues can be very subtle. While I have tried very hard not to make reference to my own family in this book, I trust my late wife would have forgiven me this one exception. I grew up in a very quiet family with one sibling. My wife had six siblings and, naturally, she had to speak louder to be heard. Early on in our marriage whenever my wife would raise her voice, this triggered off an unconscious reaction on my part to withdraw and cut off communication. Thankfully, we have worked that out over the years. However, I cannot stress enough the importance of carefully looking at all aspects of your experiences in your family of origin with special emphasis on family structure and patterns of communication and to be vigilant toward any underlying control struggles.

As noted in Chapter 7, Glasser addressed the relationship between control and behavior in his book *Stations of the Mind*. Remember that Control Theory demonstrated that our behaviors are motivated by our perceptions rather than being controlled by external factors and that as human beings we are always "controlling" for something. What we are controlling for is determined by our perception of what we want or need. In order to influence or change another's behavior we need to find out what he/she is controlling for. This requires a willingness to listen and be open to what we might hear – "seek first to understand".

Guilt

No discussion of parenting would be complete without mentioning guilt. Guilt is a powerful emotion which can not only produce anxiety and depression but can strongly influence our behavior. It is likely to be experienced by most, if not all parents at various times in child-rearing. While "guilt free" parenting has been promised by some and may seem like a worthy ideal, I believe it is much healthier to accept that we all may do (or not do) or say things we later regret and may feel guilty about. While some guilt is normal and even helpful at times, excessive guilt can become quite problematic. Obsessing about our "sins" of commission or omission and wishing we could undo them can seriously impair our functioning as parents. Parents who experience excessive guilt often end up questioning their judgment and ability to make decisions. It is important to realize that guilt is inversely related to competence. Briefly put, the more competent we are, the less guilt we will experience and the more guilty we feel, the less competent we will be.

A potentially harmful situation which I have observed more than once is when parents consciously or unconsciously use guilt as a means of motivating or attempting to control their children. While this may appear to work in the short run, there are a number of undesirable side effects. Children quickly pick up on this and use it in turn on their parents. For example, if a child is compared to a better behaved or more successful peer or sibling, it may not be too long before they are comparing their parents to a more ideal adult role model or family. But even if this form of counter manipulation doesn't occur, using guilt as a way to motivate or control children is simply not helpful to their emerging sense of self.

Where does excessive guilt come from? Perhaps our parents or teachers used it on us and we are less than consciously reliving our childhood. More likely the source of excessive guilt is what we are telling ourselves about ourselves as parents. If we have unrealistic or perfectionistic perceptions of parenting, we are sure to fall short of these ideals and experience excessive guilt. We also may have unrealistic expectations for our children and feel guilty when they seem to be falling short. On the other hand, if we acknowledge and accept the inherent challenges in parenting and our own imperfections, we can more rationally evaluate our efforts. I suggest we carefully monitor our self-talk and challenge any irrational or unrealistic beliefs or statements we may be telling ourselves.

Remember Peck's observation regarding the importance of determining what we are and are not responsible for in life. While we naturally feel responsible for our children, feeling or acting as if we are totally responsible is not helpful for them or us. When various occupations are compared as to levels of stress, air traffic controllers are usually high on the list. The reason given is the controller feels responsible for landing the plane but obviously is not flying it. I believe this is analogous to parenting. We feel responsible but we don't control the outcome. While parents need to act responsibly, acting or thinking in an overly responsible way is not in the best interest of them or their children. Dr. Hans Selye, the Austrian physician, who in 1936 identified the general adaptation syndrome and was seen as the foremost medical authority on stress noted "every living being must look out for itself first of all. There is no example in nature of a creature guided exclusively by altruism and the desire to protect others. In fact, a code of universal altruism would be highly immoral, since it would cause others to look out more for us than for themselves."

Selye offers the following advice: "Be an altruistic egoist. Do not try to suppress the natural instinct of all living beings to look after themselves first. Yet the wish to be of some use, to do some good to others, is also natural. We are social beings, and everybody wants somehow to earn respect and gratitude. You must be useful to others. This gives you the greatest degree of safety, because no one wishes to destroy a person who is useful[7]".

The message to parents: take care of yourself, strive for greater competence, make yourself helpful (but not too helpful), identify irrational beliefs or expectations about parenting and challenge them as they occur, relax and enjoy the journey.

Prayer

Often when attempting to gain control over difficult situations, some parents turn to prayer. There is a prayer called the serenity prayer which has become widely adopted by those in twelve step recovery programs. I believe it can be very helpful for parents as well. It goes something like this: Lord grant me the SERENITY to accept the things I cannot change, the COURAGE to change the things I can, and the WISDOM to know the difference.

Speaking of prayer, psychologists have finally acknowledged the fact that we have spiritual needs as well as mental and psychological needs. The general conclusion by those who have done research in this area is that if we believe when we pray that someone is listening to our prayers, there can be significant psychological benefits. Prayer can also help us to remain calm and "centered" at times of crisis. I would encourage parents not to underestimate the importance of prayer. One of the reasons I believe strongly in the power of prayer is because I am convinced that my mother's prayers saved me from potential disaster on more than one occasion. Since this is not an autobiography, I will spare you the details but Mom and her rosary beads worked overtime during my formative years.

Some time ago I had a discussion about prayer with a priest friend of mine. He asked me what I ask for when I pray. I told him I usually ask for strength, courage, and wisdom in addition to whatever specific concerns I have at that time. He told me I did not have to keep asking for strength, courage, and wisdom. God heard me the first time. He suggested I might try asking for recognition and acceptance instead. I took his advice and have found it to be very helpful. I would suggest parents who pray consider trying this approach as well.

Recognition

What do we need to recognize? Obviously, we need to be fully aware of the importance of striving to be responsible parents and the wonderful opportunities parenting provides. The potential rewards and consequences of parenting have already been discussed. However, I believe it is equally important to recognize the difficulties inherent in the parenting process. If we believe things should be relatively easy and always go well for us and our children, we will be angry and resentful when this is not the case. Conversely, if we recognize and accept the difficulties associated with parenting, it will actually become less difficult. As I previously noted, the first of Buddha's "Four Noble Truths" is "Life is Suffering." Peck paraphrases this with "Life is difficult." He elaborates, "Once we truly know that life is difficult – once we truly understand and accept it – then life is no longer difficult. Because once it is accepted, the fact that life is difficult no longer matters". As Peck, Glasser and others have noted, most of us, particularly those with serious emotional problems, do not fully accept that life is truly difficult. Albert Ellis demonstrated how the "shouldisms;" for example, "Life should be easy" or "Children should always listen" can lead to irrational beliefs, emotional distress, and ineffective parenting.

I suggest simply that substituting the word parenting for life in the above statement will provide an important part of the acknowledgement needed for effective parenting. Peck further states, "Life [parenting – my reference] is a series of problems. Do we want to moan about them or solve them? Do we want to teach our children to solve them?" I believe we need to challenge any idealistic ideas we have about parenting and adopt a perspective that allows us to prepare for the inevitable difficulties as they arise. Many parents go to great lengths to make life very pleasant and stress free for their children. This can leave them ill prepared for coping with the problems that they are likely to encounter. I realize this point has already been made earlier in this book. However, the importance of acknowledging whether we are truly preparing our children for the realities of life cannot be overstated.

A number of mental health professional have recently noted that in the pursuit of happiness for their children, many parents go to extremes to prevent them from experiencing disappointment or failure. They question whether children who have not experienced anxiety, due to their parents almost Herculean efforts to protect them from it, will be prepared to deal with the inevitable anxiety they will face as an adult. Don Kindler, a child psychologist at Harvard in his book *Too Much of a Good Thing: Raising Children of Character* points out that children need to develop a psychological immunity. If they are protected from experiencing normal stressors and painful feelings, they will not develop this immunity.

Acceptance

As previously noted, acceptance always begins with self-acceptance, which in turn requires careful self-evaluation. What are my strengths and weaknesses as a parent, as a spouse? We also need to accept our spouses and our children as they are, rather than how we would like them to be and recognize their unique abilities, talents and interests. I have worked with some unhappy adults who followed their parents' plans for success for them rather than discovering their own plans. Fortunately, most were able to make career or lifestyle changes, but not without a good deal of difficulty. Choice Theory tells us parenting does not give us the right to unfairly impose our will on our children or to destroy their dreams. Glasser advises that we keep our pictures of what we want our children to become general. Otherwise, we may push them to achieve goals for us rather than for them. I heartily agree.

Advice

When I was in graduate school one of the controversial issues in counseling and therapy was advice giving. The client-centered model, also frequently referred to as the "non-directive" approach, cautioned against advice giving. This model believed clients essentially had to come to their own insights and define their own goals, etc. The other prominent approach at that time (the "trait and factor" or "directive" approach) held that advice giving, if based on an accurate assessment of the client's situation, was appropriate and necessary. Coming out of this educational environment, many psychologists and counselors were very reluctant to offer advice. In my own practice I resolved this issue by trying very hard not to give advice until I know the person well enough to fully understand the ramifications of this advice for the client and any significant others.

The only real exception was in crisis situations where the immediate situation necessitated very direct action.

It was especially important for me to consider that advice given to parents regarding difficulties with their children be given with an understanding of its impact on the larger family system. For example, telling parents who are enmeshed with their children to spend more time with them would not be helpful. Nor would telling parents who are emotionally distant from their children to take a "tougher" approach. By thinking systemically, we can evaluate how any changes in our parenting would impact the overall family as well as the parent/child relationship. As previously noted, I believe as parents we need to be "thinking systems" at all times. If we have a good understanding of how each of the various subsystems are working, we can anticipate how changing one part of the system will affect the other parts. Remember, any real change in a system will require all other parts of that system to accommodate to the change.

There is good advice available to parents (hopefully this book contains some). However, proceed cautiously when acting on "tips" or pat solutions to problems you may be experiencing. If, in a two-parent family, you decide to institute changes, be certain both of you agree on doing so.

Above and Beyond

In addition to the obvious personal reasons for raising responsible children, I strongly believe parents have an overall responsibility to the larger social system. This responsibility includes raising children who are polite, morally well grounded, industrious, productive and sensitive to the needs of others.

The above statement may sound a bit "preachy," but I have spent most of my career dealing with individuals and families experiencing a multitude of problems. Many of these problems reflected family dysfunction and corresponding lack of responsible behavior. Family therapy training has helped me to not place the total blame on parents. Remember the concept of circular rather than linear causality. Certainly, other variables outside the families' control have been contributing factors as well. However, it is my belief that somewhere in these multigenerational family systems, individuals in key positions (within or outside of the family) were either unable or unwilling to provide the necessary responsible leadership. Note the word leadership rather than control.

In our modern competitive society, I believe many families have lost the sense of the higher order connections and obligations alluded to above. I believe one way to address many of the problems of our society is to teach our children from the earliest stage of readiness to develop a sense of awareness to the needs of others and to encourage them to reach out to those in need.

The discussion of empathy in an earlier chapter clearly pointed out that its roots are present very early in life. These can be readily nurtured by parents who are alert and empathetic themselves. I believe opportunities to do so abound. I am reminded of a family trip to Florida many years ago with our three young children. Interstate 95 was not fully completed and it was necessary to take a number of detours. On one of these side roads, we passed a very poor neighborhood. A little girl was sweeping the dirt porch of her home. Our older daughter, not quite six years old, saw the girl and told us, "When I grow up, I want to come down and help these poor people." While she doesn't live in the South, our daughter has always been very concerned about helping others and very generous in her efforts. I really don't remember exactly how we responded to her statement but I'm hoping we offered something positive. Looking back at this event, what a wonderful teaching moment! As noted above, I believe moments such as these occur frequently with our children. We need to act on these opportunities!

One of the basic premises of this book is that in order to

consistently promote responsible behavior in our children we need functional family systems. However, families may, at times, need additional help for a variety of reasons. Unfortunately, often that help is not readily available. Parents need to be persistent and assertive as advocates for their children. It is important for parents not to be intimidated by educational or helping professionals. In consulting with teachers and administrators regarding working with parents, I always stressed the need for them to be aware of the potential intimidation factor present for parents and to work to reduce this in their parent contacts.

Some parents are reluctant to ask for help, particularly from mental health professionals. There is still somewhat of a stigma in the minds of some and they see asking for help from a mental health professional as a sign of weakness, or perhaps failure as a parent. On the contrary, I have always admired parents who had the courage to come to me for help and I told them so.

There is a critical shortage of mental health providers, especially in the public sector and a definite lack of funding support by federal and state governments. The net result is that efforts at treating and remediating mental disorders fall well short of ideal.

Nicholas Kristof, in a January 7, 2014 editorial in the *New York Times* pointed out that we, as a society, hugely underinvest in mental health services. He noted, "Children in particular don't get treated nearly enough. The American Journal of Psychiatry reports that, of children ages 6 to 17 who need mental health services, 80% don't get help. Racial and ethnic minorities are even more underserved." Unfortunately, our current political leaders are less than supportive of mental health programs and funding.

A logical alternative to remediating problems would be to make prevention a higher priority. Interestingly enough, as earlier noted, Dr. Robinson referred to his work with parents as Preventive Psychiatry. I strongly agree that parent education should be an integral part of any efforts aimed at the prevention of emotional and behavioral disorders.

The Mental Health/Mental Retardation Act of 1963 was the last bill signed into law by President John F. Kennedy before his assassination. This act mandated the establishment of community mental health centers throughout the United States. These centers were *required* to provide a variety of programs including preventive programs. The preventive work was assigned to Consultation and Education departments (C&E). I served as the director of one of these C&E programs from 1977 to 1982. Our focus was on designing and implementing primary and secondary prevention programs as well as consulting to schools, day care centers, agencies, etc. I was fortunate to have a number of very talented professionals working with me and I am proud of our accomplishments. Many of our efforts directly involved parents. For example, meeting with parents of children at Kindergarten registration and offering them participation in group sessions aimed at helping them to better understand the educational process and encouraging more collaboration with their schools. Teachers and administrators consistently cited a number of positive outcomes from these groups. Follow up studies showed that parents who participated continued to be more involved in their children's education.

Another program involving two elementary schools and one high school significantly reduced chronic absenteeism and tardiness in all three schools. Obviously, we would not have been able to achieve this success without obtaining parent involvement. We consulted to numerous daycare centers and provided parent education programs through these centers. Again, follow up evaluations were very positive. I do not intend to go into great detail describing all of our programs. However, these programs provided ample evidence that helping parents to feel more competent in their child rearing can produce numerous benefits. I don't expect C&E programs to rise from the "ashes" and reappear anytime soon. I do believe, however, that much can be learned and borrowed from the work of the many C&E initiatives throughout the United States, particularly those involving parent education and support. Hopefully individuals making programmatic and funding decisions will come to this realization and we will see an increase in well designed, readily available parent education programs.

A comment by Eve Sullivan, founder of the Parents Forum in Cambridge, Massachusetts (*USA Today*, February 25, 2013) echoes these sentiments: "Instead of pushing formal schooling into early childhood, let's consider offering universal parenting education to the extent that we can prepare parents for the complex and ever-changing responsibilities of raising a child, we will have a better chance at reducing the financial and personal toll of young people's depression, alcohol, drug abuse and other behavioral problems. At the same time, we will help them achieve success in school."

Works Cited

Nichols, M. P. (1988). *The Power of the family*. New York, NY: Simon & Schuster.

Peck, M. S. (1978). *The road less traveled*. New York, NY: Simon & Schuster.

Selye, H. (1981). Introduction. In Glasser, W., *Stations of the mind*. New York, NY: Harper & Row.

Niebur, R. (1943) *Serenity Prayer*. Used in a sermon at Heath Evangelical Union Church, Heath, MA.

10

Summary and Final Thoughts

My overall goal in writing this book was to present some information, beliefs and insights which I believe would be helpful to parents and those who may become parents. The underlying principles presented were meant to be consistent with those that guided Dr. Robinson through his long and remarkably successful career as a pediatrician and parent educator. I have also shared some insights and observations from other respected sources and my own experiences in working with parents and families. I shared with you my belief that there are certain behaviors that are crucial in the process of becoming responsible parents and raising responsible kids. If by so doing, I have made parenting seem like an onerous task requiring almost superhuman powers, I sincerely apologize. Perhaps I have not spent enough time identifying and focusing on the many thoroughly enjoyable aspects of parenting. Again, I apologize if that is the case. What I would really like to do is leave you with a few ideas that you might incorporate into your day to day parenting. I fully realize that I have no control over whether you agree with these ideas or whether any suggestions are implemented. Consistent with the principles of choice theory, I can only provide information.

When Dr. Robinson conducted his clinical research, he

incorporated only the things that worked into his parent education or preventive psychiatry approach as he called it. I am attempting to do the same thing i.e., sharing with you the things that I have learned and implemented that turned out to be truly helpful to parents, both in preventing and in solving problems. I would like to briefly review the information I offered. I learned long ago that my attempting to "reinvent the wheel" was neither necessary nor productive. As a result, as you can see, I have borrowed liberally from a variety of sources in addition to Dr. Robinson as well as my own experience in presenting my suggestions to parents.

We began with Glasser's insightful statements about what constituted responsible behavior and his belief that the truly responsible person finds ways of meeting his/her needs without depriving others of the right to meet their needs. Glasser's emphasis on personal responsibility laid the groundwork for a number of very successful approaches to treatment, education, and prevention of mental disorders. In short, Glasser suggested that if we wanted to feel good, we should do good things, as individuals and as parents. I believe that if we accept and adopt Glasser's definition of responsibility we will be on our way to parent responsibly.

Scott Peck's discussion regarding the need for discipline, particularly self-discipline followed. His views regarding honesty and self-discipline, are in my opinion, particularly powerful. He also offered very valuable insights into how we might help our children develop self-discipline. For Peck, the primary role for parents is to promote their children's spiritual growth and to teach them how to effectively solve problems. Both Glasser and Peck stressed the need for finding the proper combination of love and discipline in our parenting. Peck pointed out that love is not a feeling but rather an activity and defined love as: "the will to extend one's self for the purpose of nurturing one's own or another's spiritual growth." He also dispelled some of the more popular myths about love and stressed the importance of balance in our lives.

I am certain that virtually all of the parents reading this book truly love their children. However, I have found that asking ourselves from time to time if our love meets Peck's definition can be very helpful. Peck also highlights the importance (and difficulty) of discerning what we are and are not responsible for in life, both as individuals and parents.

Daniel Goleman provided an understanding of how our neuroanatomy can significantly affect our functioning as both individuals and as parents. In *Emotional Intelligence*, he pointed out that there are two memory systems in our brain, one for rational functioning and an emotional memory system that "can act independently of the neocortex." He explains that the emotional system, which can be triggered in milliseconds by the amygdala, "is far quicker than the rational mind- springing into action without pausing for a moment to consider what it is doing." When we are unable to activate the neocortical process that usually keeps our emotional responses in balance, we have been emotionally hijacked. I believe as parents we need to be able to identify when we feel we are beginning to lose emotional control and develop ways of responding to our children that will not feed into a conflict cycle with them. I have taught a number of clients diaphragmatic breathing techniques, which I highly recommend when you feel yourself getting upset. Glasser suggests "if you feel yourself beginning to panic, slow down, count to 10 and sit on your hands."

Further, "the emotional mind reacts to the present as though it were in the past." When some feature of an event seems similar to an emotionally charged memory from the past by triggering the feelings that went with the remembered event." As individuals and as parents we need to become aware of those stored images and memories and experiences that can trigger an exaggerated or inappropriate emotional response. Obviously, this is most likely to happen during a real (or imagined) crisis. Not reacting inappropriately or overreacting requires emotional intelligence. Goleman identifies emotional intelligence as a key set of abilities, "such as being able to motivate oneself and persist in the face of frustration; to control impulse and delay gratification, to regulate one's moods and keep distress from swamping the ability to think; to empathize and to hope."

Many efforts at helping parents do not, in my opinion, give sufficient attention to the fact that parents, like all human beings, cannot always function rationally. As noted above, I believe we need to realize that and devise strategies for dealing with those occasions when emotional hijacking is most likely to occur. Goleman also cited research indicating the key role that empathy plays in successful parenting. These findings show that empathy builds on self-awareness. The more open we are to our own feelings the more empathetic we can be. We also need to remain calm enough to identify the subtle verbal and non-verbal signs of feelings in others, particularly our spouses and children. Goleman notes, "Family life is our first school for emotional learning." Modeling emotional intelligence can powerfully influence our children.

In reflecting on a number of research studies focusing on parental behavior and brain development, Goleman summarized "there are very different emotional habits instilled by parents whose discipline includes empathy on the one hand, or self-absorbed parents who ignore a child's distress or who discipline by yelling and hitting."

I shared my belief that many attempts to help or advise parents did not fully consider the larger context in which parenting occurs and that consistently responsible parenting requires a functional family system. Some basic principles of systems theory were presented along with structural family therapy concepts. Murray Bowen's theory of individuation/differentiation was also discussed. He believed that in order to grow up emotionally we need to negotiate our separateness from our family of origin without cutting off relations with family members. Bowen also believed that a lack of individuation can be passed on from generation to generation and stressed the importance of carefully exploring and understanding our family of origin. The concept of families as developmental systems was also briefly presented.

Also as previously noted, I believe parents need to take a leadership role in establishing and maintaining functional family systems. Since systems carry out their functions through their various subsystems, guidelines for assessing and monitoring the functionality of those subsystems were presented and criteria for healthy family functioning were offered. In addition to the family structure, ongoing patterns of communication also need to be assessed and monitored. Several suggestions for effective communication were offered, including those by Ginott and Gordon. Structure and communication are, in my opinion, interchangeable.

I shared my belief that we are influenced (but not controlled) in numerous ways by our past and present experiences within our families of origin. Hopefully you will take the time to complete the FOS if you have not already done so and follow the suggestions for reviewing the results. I have found that in a two-parent family, if both parents do this individually and discuss the results the exercise can be well worth the time it requires. The exercise can, of course, also be helpful for single parents.

Glasser's most recent theory, choice theory, was discussed. He based his formulations primarily upon control theory, a theory that focuses on understanding ways in which living organisms control what happens to them. Essentially this theory describes the brain as an input control system which attempts to help us fulfill our needs. Its basic principle is that we strive to control for what we perceive, not what actually exists. Control theory and Choice theory also stress the fact that we are internally rather than externally controlled.

A number of suggestions were offered for readers who may want to become "Choice theory parents". Since most of us grew up with external control, I find parents often have difficulty making this shift. I can tell you from my experience that most parents I have worked with found this approach to be very helpful. Choice theory teaches that establishing and maintaining a positive ongoing relationship with our children is one of a parent's most important tasks. In helping parents to do the "work" of the relationship, I have used the analogy of the parent-child relationship being seen as a living organism. Like all living organisms, it needs to be nurtured, fed and attended to and given the freedom and opportunity to reach its full growth potential. Remember, the relationship take precedence over always being right and punishment does not permanently change behavior.

Steven Covey noted that responsibility is really two words, response and ability. Rather than simply responding reflexively to stimuli as animals do, we can, due to the unique human characteristics of self- awareness, conscience, imagination and independent will, choose our responses. In reviewing years of success literature, Covey identified the character ethic as the real foundation for success. Individuals who followed the character ethic were referred to as "principle centered." He listed a number of characteristics of principle centered people, including "things like integrity, humility, fidelity, temperance, courage, justice, patience, industry, simplicity, modesty and the Golden Rule." When parents are principle centered rather than relying on techniques or gimmicks, they can be proactive rather than reactive in their dealings with their children. Covey recommends developing personal and family mission statements. Asking ourselves what kind of person and parent do I want to be can help us to see parenting (and life) as internally rather than externally controllable. Covey's view that we are internally controlled is consistent with Glasser's beliefs.

I included a discussion of the emotional development of children, citing the work of the psychoanalyst, Erik Erickson. Most parents are truly amazed when they realize the depth of their child's psychodynamic experiences. I noted in particular, the series of developmental crises which need to be resolved in order to function on a healthy emotional level. I believe it is very important that parents become aware of and sensitive to the various aspects of psychodynamic and psychosocial development.

I shared with you Dr. Robinson's specific approach to working with children and parents. His clinical research and the comments of the teachers and counselors which first made me aware of him and his work and are testimony to the effectiveness of his approach. My home was approximately thirty miles from Dr. Robinson's but we worked in different metropolitan areas. If it were not for the very positive unsolicited statements about the "Robinson Kids," I would never had met this remarkable man.

I believe that despite the fact that the information in this book comes from a variety of sources, there is a consistent theme. Amazingly to me, this theme was reflected in Dr. Robinson's work. He stressed responsibility and honesty and believed parents' primary goal should be helping their children learn self-discipline. His recommendations included many of the behaviors and thoughts that were consistent with emotional intelligence. His awareness of the need for monitoring healthy family functioning was reflected in insisting upon a unified approach by both parents in child rearing in two parent families. This is obviously consistent with the need to maintain functional parental and spousal subsystems. He stressed the need for appropriate generational boundaries. In my conversations with him he frequently decried the fact that children are handled too much. He also believed in parents not intervening too readily in sibling subsystem disputes. He believed that it was very important for children to have chores and that they needed this responsibility to help them to develop a sense of self-worth. He recommended non punitive forms of discipline (e.g. time out) which if correctly applied in childhood would preclude the need for reliance on more harsh forms of discipline later on. He stressed the importance of maintaining a positive parent and children relationship but not being overly responsible for them. This is clearly reflected in his philosophy of *judicious neglect*.

Dr. Robinson told me he didn't believe in "sugar coating" or "schmoozing" with parents to get them to like him. He pointed out that parenting is by nature difficult and challenging and that it required courage, patience, and persistence. He told parents that if they wanted their children to be self-disciplined and emotionally mature, they needed to consistently model these behaviors. He stressed openness in communication and a non-hostile sense of humor. I sincerely believe that if his specific recommendations are followed from day one, both children and parents would benefit greatly. I believe his "preventive psychiatry" approach was consistent with Choice Theory, which focuses on *preventing* problems in parent child relationships.

In summary, if we want our children to grow to become responsible adults, which I have found to be most parents' primary goal, what do we need to do? The short answer is to accept responsibility for our behavior. Glasser believed the word behavior is used too narrowly. He noted that the dictionary definition of behavior as the way of conducting oneself did not fully capture the dynamic interaction of the various components of behavior. He suggested we use the term "total behavior," which included our actions, our thoughts, our feelings and our physiological responses to our actions, thoughts and feelings. Of these four components of our total behavior, we can really only control two, our thoughts and our behaviors. Our feelings and physiological responses, including our brain chemistry, are largely controlled by what we do and what we think. Since human beings are intrinsically active, we are always doing something. I believe the most important questions we can ask ourselves at any given time are what am I choosing to do and what am I choosing to think? Are my actions and behaviors consistent with my values, goals, and ideals. A number of research studies have found that people's actions are very often not consistent with their expressed values. I recommended asking yourself what it is that you are and are not responsible for and I encouraged you to think "systems." I also recommend you monitor your thoughts and challenge any unrealistic or perfectionist beliefs about parenting. In addition to acting and thinking we are always feeling something, although we may not always be aware of our feelings.

I believe we need to monitor these feelings in terms of whether they are helpful or harmful to us as individuals and as parents. Along with pure feelings, which are usually brief and transitory, we have what Glasser referred to as feeling behaviors. Choice theory tells us we choose these behaviors. One of my standard therapeutic strategies was to help clients understand their feeling behaviors. I would tell them that when what we want (our reference perception) is not realistic or attainable, we have a number of choices. We can feel sorry for ourselves (a natural response), we can get angry about it (also a natural response), we can worry and dwell on it (also understandable) or we can tell ourselves there must be something I can do to make things better for myself. I called the last choice the "responsible" choice.

Emerson said that thinking is the hardest work of all that's why so few do it. Thomas Watson, the legendary CEO of IBM required all employees to have THINK signs in their offices or work places, reminding them of the necessity to do just that. Many felt this was crucial to the spectacular success of the company. I believe we do need to remind ourselves to think. There is a college near where I live and where I take my daily (almost) walk, Clark Summit University. They have flags attached to lamp posts throughout the campus as reminders to students (and others). Currently the signs are: *Think Biblically, Grow Spiritually, Serve Faithfully, and Major in Making a Difference.* Since the laws of remembering and forgetting apply to parenting as well as all other aspects of our lives, having visual or auditory reminders may be a very good idea for parents.

As our children grow and develop certainly our approach to parenting has to change somewhat. However, if we remain true to the principles of responsible parenting, we will be able to adapt to these changing demands. Having a healthy, functional family system will also give us the flexibility needed to respond to these demands. I believe that while we are helping our children grow in responsibility, they are also providing us with numerous opportunities for our own spiritual and emotional growth.

Glasser believed that our children need us to be responsible. "The parents must understand that the child needs responsible parents and that taking the responsible course will <u>never</u> permanently alienate the child. An appreciation of this one simple fact greatly aids parents in teaching their children responsibility." He continues, "When discipline is reasonable and understandable and when the parents' own behavior is consistent with their demands on the child, he will love and respect them even though his surface attitude may not always show it."

Some Final Thoughts

Although we can continue to be helpful to and supportive of our children throughout their lives, we really only get one shot at basic parenting.

While is it reasonable for us to hope that our children find happiness in their own right, if we attempt to protect them from any form of unhappiness while they are with us, we may not be preparing them for dealing with the inevitable "ups" and "downs" of adult living.

Remember, parenting occurs in a multigenerational family content. An awareness of this can help to deal with difficult parent-child issues.

Striving to be perfect parents never works, responsible kids only require "good enough," not perfect parenting.

Dr. Robinson believed, as do I, that the greatest gift we can give our children is a level of self-discipline that will enable them to make responsible choices throughout their lives.

As I am nearing the completion of this book, we are in the midst of the COVID-19 Pandemic. I can't imagine a better example of the need for people with a level of self-discipline necessary to observe the various rules and restrictions and the empathy or compassion needed to truly care for their fellow human beings. Let's hope there are a lot of former Robinson Kids out there. Seriously, we need to recognize that we are raising our children to able to cope with the many challenges and uncertainties they are likely to face.

Keep in mind Peck's definition of love in your parenting that is, any activity that has as its purpose fostering out children's emotional and spiritual growth.

Finally, remember the need to discern what we are and are not responsible for as parents. We might ask ourselves the following questions: Do we want to teach our children how to solve their problems or try to solve all of their problems for them? Do we want to protect our children from all adversity and disappointment or do we want to help them to learn how to deal with them and develop the "psychological immunity" needed to help them deal with the adversity and disappointments they may experience as adults?

I sincerely wish the very best to every parent or would be parent who reads this book. Thank you for the opportunity to share this information with you.

Works Cited

Glasser, W. (1985). *Control Theory*. New York, NY: Harper & Row.
Peck, S. (1978). *The Road Less Traveled*. New York, NY: Simon & Schuster.
Goleman, W. (1965). *Emotional Intelligence*. New York, NY: Bontam Books.

APPENDIX

OFFICE HOURS BY APPOINTMENT TELEPHONE: 288-1359
NO HOURS ON FRIDAY IF NO ANSWER, CALL: 824-9881

JOSEPH ROBINSON, M.D.

47 PIERCE STREET
KINGSTON, PA. 18704

John J 10/17/78

Ht = 45 3/4"
Wt. = 42#

DPT due 10/79

Home menu +
schedule

Chores!!

TELEPHONE HOURS: 8-11 A.M. DAILY EXCEPT FRIDAY

OFFICE HOURS BY APPOINTMENT TELEPHONE 288-1359
NO HOURS ON FRIDAY IF NO ANSWER, CALL 824-9881

JOSEPH ROBINSON, M. D.

47 PIERCE STREET
KINGSTON, PA.

David K 10/21/74

Ht: 22 1/2"
Wt: 11# 4 oz

Rotate grains +
increase amt
steadily.

Cereal + 4 oz formula → thick

Start vegetables:
Try all
Test each, 3 days
at lunch
all he'll take
Before bottle.

TELEPHONE HOURS: 8-11 A.M. DAILY EXCEPT FRIDAY

OFFICE HOURS BY APPOINTMENT TELEPHONE 288-1359
NO HOURS ON FRIDAY IF NO ANSWER, CALL 824-9881

JOSEPH ROBINSON, M. D.

47 PIERCE STREET
KINGSTON, PA.

David K 12/21/74

Ht = 25 1/4"
Wt. = 16# 2 oz

Schedulize:
In crib, alone 4 hrs
between feedings +
12 hrs after supper

Meats: Try all
Test each 2 days
at lunch
meat
veget
bottle
Supper - cereal
meat
bottle

TELEPHONE HOURS: 8-11 A.M. DAILY EXCEPT FRIDAY

OFFICE HOURS BY APPOINTMENT TELEPHONE 288-1359
NO HOURS ON FRIDAY IF NO ANSWER, CALL 824-9881

JOSEPH ROBINSON, M. D.

47 PIERCE STREET
KINGSTON, PA.

David K 2/15/75

Ht: 26 1/2"
Wt: 18# 15 oz

3rd DPT
again

Continue antibiotic

Regular milk

Custards, pudding,
+ jello as dessert

Meat 2x daily

orange juice

Wean from
milk off
3 oz daily

TELEPHONE HOURS: 8-11 A.M. DAILY EXCEPT FRIDAY

OFFICE HOURS BY APPOINTMENT   TELEPHONE 288-1350
NO HOURS ON FRIDAY   IF NO ANSWER, CALL 824-0881

JOSEPH ROBINSON, M. D.
47 PIERCE STREET
KINGSTON, PA.

David R.   11/1/77

HX = 37¼"
2HX = 32#

DPT due 3/78
vitamin
meat — 2x daily
nap + 12 hr /night
discipline —
Corner stand

OFFICE HOURS BY APPOINTMENT   TELEPHONE: 288-1350
NO HOURS ON FRIDAY   IF NO ANSWER, CALL: 824-0881

JOSEPH ROBINSON M.D.
47 PIERCE STREET
KINGSTON, PA. 18704

David Kennedy   10/9/79

HX = 43"
2HX = 40½

Resume vitamin
E plus.

Same eating regime
only water between
meals
12 hrs sleep/night

Telephone Hours: 8-11 A.M. Daily Except Friday

Telephone Hours: 8-11 A.M.

REFERENCES

American College Health Association. "Emotional Problem Experienced by College Students" cited in Lythcott-Haines *How to Raise an Adult*.

Bandura, A. *Self Efficacy* cited in Lythcott-Haines *How to Raise an Adult*.

Bowen, M. (1978). *Family Therapy in Clinical Practice*. New York, NY: Jason Aronson.

Carter, B., & McGoldrick, M. (Eds.). (1988). *The changing family life cycle*. New York, NY: Gardner Press.

Cline, F. & Fay, J. "Helicopter Parents" cited in Lythcott-Haines *How to Raise an Adult*.

Covey, S. (1989). *The Seven Habits of Highly Effective People*. New York, NY: Simon & Schuster.

Davidson, M. (1983). *Uncommon sense: The life & thought of Ludwig Von Bertalanffy*. Los Angeles, CA: J. P. Tarcher, Inc.

Erikson, E. H. (1994). *Identity & the Life Cycle*. New York - London: W. W. Norton & Company

Emerson, R.W. in *Intellect in the Great Thoughts*. 1985. New York, NY: Ballentine Books

Framo, J. L. (1992). *Family-of-origin therapy: An intergenerational approach*. New York, NY: Routledge.

Ginott, H. G. (1965). *Between parent & child*. New York, NY: Avon Books.

Glasser, W. (1965). *Reality therapy.* New York, NY: Harper & Row.
Glasser, W. (1981). *Stations of the Mind.* New York, NY: Harper & Row.
Glasser, W. (1984). *Control theory: A new explanation of how we control our lives.* New York: Harper and Row.
Glasser, W. (1998). *Choice Theory: A New Psychology of Personal Freedom.* New York, NY: Harper & Row.
Goleman, D. (1995). *Emotional intelligence.* New York, NY: Bantam Books.
Goleman, D., Boyatzis, R., McKee, A. (2013). *Primal leadership: Unleashing the power of emotional intelligence.* Boston, MA: Harvard Business Review Press.
Gordon, T. (2000). *Parent effectiveness training: The proven program for raising responsible children.* New York, NY: Three Rivers Press.
Hooven, C. & Gottman, J. as cited in Goleman, D. (1995). Emotional intelligence. New York, NY: Bantam Books.
Journal of Family Psychology. "Criteria for Adulthood" cited in Lythcott-Haines *How to Raise an Adult.*
Le Doux, J. as cited in Goleman, D. (1995). *Emotional intelligence.* New York, NY: Bantam Books.
Levone, M. "Overparenting" cited in Lythcott-Haines *How to Raise an Adult.*
Lythcott-Haines, J. (2015). *How to Raise an Adult.* New York, NY: Henry Holt & Company.
Macohy, E. & Marin, J. "Parental Types" cited in Lythcott-Haines *How to Raise an Adult.*
Minuchin, S. (1974). *Families & family therapy.* Cambridge, MA: Harvard University Press.
Mogel, W. *The Blessing of the Skinned Knee* cited in Lythcott-Haines *How to Raise an Adult.*
Nichols, M. P. (1988). *The Power of the family.* New York, NY: Simon & Schuster.

Niebur, R. (1943) *Serenity Prayer.* Used in a sermon at Heath Evangelical Union Church, Heath, MA

Peck, M. S. (1978). *The Road less traveled.* New York, NY: Simon & Schuster.

Salovey, P. & Mayer, J. as cited in Goleman, D. (1995). *Emotional intelligence.* New York, NY: Bantam Books.

Selye, H. (1981). Introduction. In Glasser, W., *Stations of the mind.* New York, NY: Harper & Row.

Stern, D. as cited in Goleman, D. (1995). *Emotional intelligence.* New York, NY: Bantam Books.

Thomas, G. (1970). *Parent effectiveness training.* New York, NY: Random House.

Lightning Source UK Ltd.
Milton Keynes UK
UKHW010640180121
377244UK00001B/245